Let's Sit Down and Talk

ALSO BY MARVIN BERENSON

Fiction
The World Beyond Time
Woodson's World
The Twin's Soul
The Search for Arthur Kingsley
The Tipping Point: The Year 2030

Nonfiction
A Guide to Healthy Relationships
Inspiring Tales of Psychotherapy
Awakening Your Creativity
Dynamic Retirement

Let's Sit Down and Talk

ABOUT A HAPPIER AND HEALTHIER YOU

A Collection of Articles for Seniors

Rossmoor News Health Columnist

MARVIN BERENSON M.D.

Let's Sit Down and Talk

Copyright © 2020 Marvin Berenson

All rights are reserved

All rights reserved. No part of this book may be reproduced, distributed or transmitted in any form or by any means or by information or retrieval systems without written permission of the author, except for the inclusion of brief quotations in a review.

ISBN: 978-0-9700885-7-4

Published by

Big Hat Press
Lafayette, California
www.bighatpress.com

*I dedicate this book to my
loving wife, Irene Cole Berenson.*

TABLE OF CONTENTS

Acknowledgments		ix
Introduction		xi
1	Belief in Yourself and the Process of Change	1
2	The Spirit of Creativity	5
3	Never Grow Old	8
4	Becoming a Poet	12
5	Adventures of the Soul	16
6	Mindfulness and Your Imagination	20
7	The Heart of Spirituality	23
8	An Easy to Use Effective Diet Program	26
9	The Complexity of Healthful Eating	30
10	Laughter	34
11	Balance: Preventing Falling	38
12	The Challenge of Control: Do Not Fall	42
13	Reckoning with Our Fears	46
14	Understanding Heart Disease	50
15	The Prevention of Heart Disease	54
16	The Prevention of Cancer	58
17	Delaying and Preventing Dementia	62
18	Overcoming the Fear of Dementia Using Mental Imagery	66
19	Are You Worried About Alzheimer's?	70
20	The Caregivers and Alzheimer's	74
21	Lightening the Caregiver's Burdens	78
22	Overcoming the Fear of Dying	82
23	The Joy of Treasure Seeking	86
24	Discoveries as a Way of Life	89
25	The Search for Love	92

26	A Rolling Leaf	95
27	All the World's a Stage	98
28	Who am I?	102
29	The Imagination	105
30	What is Truth? The Testing of Your Beliefs	109
31	How do We Truly Live the Good Life?	113
32	Authenticity and Character	117
33	I Don't Remember: Just a Senior Moment	121
34	Your Soul Soars with Music	125
35	Conquering Negativism	129
36	The End of All Negatives	133
37	Shake those Bones: You Need to Play	137
38	Say No to Procrastination	140
39	Songs of the Soul	143
40	The Art of the Bounce	146
41	Conquering Your Worries	150
42	The Bounty of Nature	154
43	Love to the Rescue	158
44	Endless Love	162
45	The Enjoyment of Solitude	166
46	Update Your Self-Care	170
47	Intimate Communication	174
48	Taking Charge of Your Life	178
49	Are You a Warrior?	182
50	Insomnia	185
51	Finding Inspiration	189
52	The Joining as I say Goodbye	192

About the Author   195

ACKNOWLEDGMENTS

I am especially grateful to our former editor, Maureen O'Rourke who offered me the *Rossmoor News* Health Column two and half years ago, and to our current editor, Ann Peterson who has continued to support the column. They have provided me with a broad-based format for my ideas and my gratitude to them is deep and heartfelt. I love Rossmoor and my favorite activity is being the *Rossmoor News* Health Columnist.

The residents of Rossmoor have contributed to the birth of many of my articles. When someone approaches me or I hear indirectly of pain or sadness in the community, my first impulse is how to help them. Many of these individuals I only know slightly or only by their desire to hear from me on a particular subject. But I do wish to also acknowledge my debt to the residents for their openness to the articles. They have been very receptive to my thoughts, imagination and special techniques for extending help to them. I always appreciate hearing from them in their frequent letters or calls and learning when someone was specifically enlightened.

When I write about animals and nature, it is natural for me to express myself in a poetic manner. When I write of hugging a tree, my imagination is speaking, but it may also be a real event. I easily approach a real live tree and share hugs, yes, share hugs for the tree is grateful for the connection and responds. However, I truly enjoy imagining a magical tree that extends its branches in a connection of love. Yes, love.

Several close friends who have helped, advised or encouraged me regarding certain articles include Joel Aberbach, a deep and brotherly friend, who is a font of information and a gentle soul who at times reached out to soothe and comfort me when I was troubled or in some doubt. Additionally, he offered me certain ideas in areas where he is expert. Shelly Kushin, a wonderful friend, with an infectious laugh, was always available for advice or to review and edit something I've written. She is someone I could depend on for her accurate evaluation and her honest opinion and reaction.

Finally, I acknowledge the continuous, highly valuable contribution of Irene, my wife. Not only was she the editor with her impeccable knowledge and judgment on all the articles but she is an advisor who I have always heeded through the years.

INTRODUCTION

For over two years, I have had the time of my life writing articles for the "Rossmoor News" Health Column. I have enjoyed reading the many letters I received from the residents informing me of the benefits and pleasures they have gained and that I have helped change their life. Such reactions have been extremely gratifying to me whose goal in life has been to help others.

I decided to gather in one place the 52 best received articles. Each week or daily for that matter, you can peer over my shoulder for ideas about the wonders of life, the many methods to find fulfillment, ways to become more creative, locating conduits to a more exciting and also to a more tranquil lifestyle.

Are you worried about heart disease, preventing cancer, dealing with the scary effects of Alzheimer's Disease? Learn about these conditions and check out my views on how to handle your feelings. I wade into the areas of spirituality, relationships, love in all its many splendors, developing friendships. Humor plays a big part in many of my articles. You must laugh to be really alive. One of my biggest affirmations is strictly a big belly laugh. Stopping clutter, overcoming procrastination, turning aloneness and sadness into solitude and inner peacefulness are other subjects I discuss.

And with my playful spirit and humor and connection with nature I write freely and frequently about our animals and birds. One of the friendly crows living in Rossmoor meets with me occasionally and offers me advice that I might have missed. You'll have to search the articles and see if I included one of our lively discussions. Other friends include tiny lizards, fluttering birds that land on my shoulder and engage in conversation, our beautiful deer and the baby fawns that wander through our park-like setting and often, oblivious of cars, join the turkeys and stroll into the street. In Rossmoor everyone watches carefully for our friendly deer nodding hello, as they pass you by.

Of course, there are thousands of dogs in Rossmoor offering uncontested love and companionship to many residents. One evening unknown to their masters and mistresses a small group gathered in a hidden alcove to discuss the deep loneliness and sadness of several of their masters and mistresses. We meet Goldie and others as they determine the best plans to help their owners.

The urban forest of Rossmoor and its nearly ten thousand residents is so special and unique that on several occasions I have been tempted to write about our utopia but stopped when the word magic appeared several times in my developing article. The residents don't need reminding that they live in a unique and magic kingdom. When I allude to my greeting and speaking with the faces in the passing clouds some people might consider that magical thinking. Whereas for me that is merely an example of how we live in nature. After all, the articles are part of a Health Column and I am determined that every article clearly describes new ways to live life more fully.

That is also the purpose of this book. Readers can pick it up and find solutions to problems and ways to become happier, more productive and more creative no matter what was the initial state of mind. It's kind of like having me in your pocket and picking me up for an intimate conversation. It might start with, "Say Marv, could you introduce me to Charlie, the friendly crow, and what about that gorgeous bird that just landed on your nose?"

1

Belief in Yourself and the Process of Change

The process of change is inevitable. From infancy to adulthood in less than two decades we change from helplessness to maturity. During our adulthood, we continue to grow and change as we navigate education, work, marriage, raising children, and finally reach retirement.

You now face an opportunity to enjoy the fruits of your final period of life. With a positive frame of mind and the willingness to open yourself to a new exciting life of activity, learning, new experiences, becoming more creative, productive, and finding new ways to love and receive love, your new life will unfold.

Belief in yourself is the essential ingredient. Most important is the belief that your self-value is heading to new heights and your entire life is now reaching a new level of fulfillment. Unlimited venues fill the palate. Painting pictures, creating sculptures, writing stories, expanding your dance skills, acting in a play and becoming more loving, giving, and helpful. Don't forget that playing golf, bocce ball and exercising are all aspects of self-improvement.

Any method that enhances such development should be welcome. You know about mindfulness, mental imagery, self-suggestion, and joining groups or clubs for mutual encouragement. Understanding about the full life cycle and how to accept the end of life that leads to a peaceful death is another area that people of all ages reflect on but especially those who are older. It is never too late to learn about a healthful and effective diet program that is strictly self-contained and requires no outside help. Finding the road to spirituality within and outside religion is another important area for development I am going to emphasize. Have you considered that laughter and living in a state of humor and fun is attainable even during a time of aging? Beyond just telling jokes it is how you look at life, how you cast away negativism, how you imbibe the merry, gleeful giggles of small children and awaken your own inner child. It can certainly be fun growing older. I can't wait until I get there myself.

These are some of the subjects I hope to address in the coming months to help you reach new heights in all your pursuits, new levels of satisfaction, enhanced creativity, productivity and greater acceptance of your aging self.

To begin our ventures into a more bountiful and healthful life I would like to introduce a simple and effective method to help you through difficult periods and more importantly to offer a method to improve your life, give you ideas to bring a new sense of spirit and vitality to your existence. We know this simple technique as the use of affirmations. People have used and repeated simple truths, encouraging words, ideas to change beliefs for as long as people have had the power to think and reflect. Children, as well as adults, use affirmations. "I am mentally strong and can't be defeated, I am smart and will be successful, I am beautiful and people respond to me, I am a lovely person and I also love myself." Most people have used these at times. We all remember the famous affirmation initiated by Emile Coué "Every day, in every way I'm getting better and better." This was widely quoted in the early part of the 20th century.

Autosuggestion, the mental ingredient at the heart of using affirmations, depends on the imagination to think up sayings that can markedly influence you. Affirmations can be repeated throughout the day in seconds. The world of affirmations depends on belief in yourself; it does not rely on mindfulness. It depends on the ideas you have. It depends on repetition. And you must want to make the change. You want to believe in yourself. They must not become clichés. They must not be said in passing when they have little consequence or meaning. You must believe what they say. And you must activate your words.

If you want to become more loving, then you have to feel it, know you want to love more and want to practice loving. Becoming more loving works better with twinkling eyes and a smile on your face. Tell yourself "I am a loving person and will share my love with others."

Others are: "Every day I will help someone in need. I will learn to live better. I will help children learn and be happy. I will help the poor. I will eat a healthier diet." The number of affirmations are legion. They lead to change. The essence of affirmation is believing and knowing that what you affirm is truly what you want to change. To foster the change you must actively assist what you specifically state. The combination of autosuggestion and active compliance with the affirmation will lead to real and lasting change. Remember your belief is essential to make it effective.

2
The Spirit of Creativity

Fulfillment comes in many guises but none as exciting and mind expanding as the opening of one's creativity. No matter what age you begin, whether you are 20, 60, 90 or even 100 you can unhesitatingly move into the beckoning arena of creativity. It is imperative that you believe in the potential that lies within you. Don't be caught up in the myth that creativity is for the young. The development of a person's innate skills and enhanced productiveness expands for many older people. The essence of opening new doors, delving into previously untried activities, exploring new venues that just days or weeks ago were shrouded in blackness is BELIEF IN ONE'S SELF. Your creativity is to be cherished and developed.

An unparalleled opportunity to reconnect with your creative self awaits you. Think back to your childhood. Remember building toys from everyday objects and playing games that took you and friends to an unknown world. You created imaginary playmates, built castles in the sky, believed in magic, talked to spirits, ghosts and magical people. You didn't try to eliminate such unrealistic games or playmates. Instead, you welcomed them into your life.

Painting a picture was another vehicle to an imaginary world. Whether you attempted to reproduce a real object on canvas or merely painted whatever feelings guided you, your painting represented your creative self. If you only painted smudges or smeared globs of paint on paper you knew what they meant. The outsider, even Mom, could only guess what the abstract painting represented. But you could describe what each segment meant. Nothing was meaningless. Your mind was your playground and using it was natural. And it all remains waiting to be rekindled. It only takes stirring your imagination and learning ways to bring it back to life.

Please join me in some exercises to stimulate your creative juices. From an almost unlimited number of ways to tap into this world, I have selected four to illustrate how your imagination will always come to your assistance as you peer unerringly into the glowing world of YOUR creativity.

WRITING POETRY: Sit quietly in a chair, close your eyes and imagine seeing a small bird fly from the sky and settle directly in front of you. What ensues is your poem. Without hesitation, you speak to it. Example. "Your feathers are a delight to my eye." The bird responds and a dialogue follows that may go on for many verses. Be spontaneous, never wonder what your words mean, but yet make them real and directed to the bird who responds with great intelligence. His first words might be: "They take me oh so high." This interaction with a bird almost always produces a charming poem. Later you can repeat this creative exercise with other animals, other birds and with inanimate objects such as trees.

Next exercise, as you remain seated with your eyes closed, go into a room and see three closed doors on one wall. You feel a great urgency to open one of the doors knowing that it will lead you to an entirely new experience and bring you face to face with a forgotten dream or open an entirely new idea for you to pursue. Whatever is behind the door you open follow your inclinations and go where your imagination takes you. If you don't like what you see try a different door. Ex., On an occasion when an older person did the exercise, she opened the door to a vista of a vast beautiful library and immediately realized how she had always wanted to return to college. Several months later, she matriculated at a nearby college.

Our third exercise will take you to the heart of a heated discussion on politics or religion or the climate or other subject and you will address the small group of people as a person with knowledge and oratory skills. In your imagination, you rise higher in your ability than ever before and know you have the capacity to bring that ability into real life. One person who did this exercise in the past decided to enter politics as a result.

Finally, our fourth exercise involves incorporating the personality, abilities, talents of an artist, musician or writer and by temporarily identifying with that person you realize a dream of becoming a highly skilled artist. By repeating this exercise over many weeks, using variations of what aspects you play out, you can develop greater skills in the art of your choice. You have merely absorbed the artistry of a mentor much as artists have done in the past by working in the workshops of other artists. You have created a mentor. And why limit yourself to only one.

Believe in your imagination and creativity. They are part of you.

3
Never Grow Old

Old age creeps up slowly, almost unseen, but it is relentless and suddenly it is there. Does it scare you? Hopefully not. Rather you should be aware of your advancing age and early in the process go to the mirror and say, "I look as young as ever and my time has come to walk into the future as a young person." Laugh at the idea of getting old and bring your humor to the table.

Am I dealing with fantasy, whimsy or denial or just closing my eyes and mind to the inevitable aging process that is approaching? Not on your life (wrong metaphor) but you get the idea. For I am now about to write that youthfulness is in you and can remain with you forever. 70's, 80's, 90's, dare I say the 100's.

So now with the pep talk out of the way I want to present the evidence of how you can imagine your future as a perpetually youthful person. What makes us young? Calendar age. Physical prowess and relatively good strength. Mental ability at its peak. Continuing to enjoy sex. All true, but the key to remain young is to change your calendar age.

What if I now claim that if you eliminate following your calendar age, then all the other examples of youthfulness can be maintained indefinitely, if you fully believe in your mind's capacity to guide and control your future. Any changes that occur will be accepted as a part of your lifecycle. Drown out any negatives that try to disrupt your positive attitude.

Once you believe that your real age is strictly your mental age, nothing will deter you from having an alive, vital and productive life as you grow older. Once you accept that you were born into this world to succeed in your efforts to find meaning and purpose, then so it will be.

No doubt, having experienced good and loving mothering and fathering will foster your development. However, some will find their paths strewn with barriers and handicaps. Others will be pushed along without any obstacles. Some will come into the world stronger and healthier than others, with different degrees of intelligence and hardiness, but all will be unique and most will be individuals capable of forging successful paths throughout their lives. Most will be willing to fight for success and actively seek love and want to give love to others. They will become increasingly aware of overcoming whatever deficiencies they carry and find ways to rise high into the world they choose.

You will learn that that having an inner sense of direction, learning to be active and self-motivated and never succumbing to a negative attitude toward life will become your mantras of living well. However, many seniors go through a phase of self-doubt, increasing passivity, fear of pursuing new goals and feeling inferior. These negative beliefs are rather commonplace and linger because the recipients, meaning those who carry them consciously, without making any effort to overcome them, close their eyes to possible solutions.

Now is the time to open your eyes to who you are. You are readying yourself to change, to grow. You are taking a deep breath and filling your lungs with the healthy breath of life that will course through your body and rattle any lazy bones or flaccid muscles. Naturally, it mostly penetrates your brain and mind for that is the locus of change.

The mind is the repository of change and insight and your wish to grow and expand. You are going to **look at any falseness** you carry, personas that hide your true self. You have a major task ahead. You must overcome your reluctance to admit your weaknesses and sense of emptiness or self-doubt you feel you carry. Those who exaggerate these traits and live a life of inferiority and futility have a special need to face their negativity. **Above all, they must not close their eyes to who they are.**

The emphasis is **always** face your negativity and strive to reduce and overcome it. No matter what degree of baggage you carry, with effort and motivation you can initiate change once faced.

As we ponder change and gather our fighting forces to overcome our negativity and obstacles to retaining our youthfulness, a new sense of enlightenment and optimism will stimulate our zeal to jump into the fray of change. You will find ways to remove the chains that stymie your mobility, break open the prison doors that prevent freedom, and remove the blindfolds that cover your eyes.

Do the following exercise daily: **Everyday** look into your mirror and **listen** to your mirror-self tell you how **young, vibrant and mentally alive** you are.

Are you rubbing your hands with anticipation?

4

Becoming a Poet

---

*"To see a world in a grain of sand,
And a heaven in a wild flower,
To hold infinity in the palm of your hand,
And Eternity in an hour."*

— *Auguries of Innocence* by William Blake

There's magic in words. The words of a poet. In 30 words, William Blake touched the deepest feelings of life, and in a brief moment of time brought us the world in a few thoughts.

Everybody has the soul of a poet. Most of us have written poems in the past and some continue today. A quatrain can be written in mere minutes or after hours of reflection. Poems of any length are written without concern for time. They tap into our deepest mental resources, our unconscious where we ferret out mysteries and insights and scenes of beauty.

Although I am tempted to offer many examples of beautiful poetry, I doubt that any reader needs any urging to try their hand at creating poetry. How do you start? With an idea, a feeling, a dream. Love, war, nature, the vicissitudes of relationships, beauty, spirituality, gustatory delights, hearth and home, children and mystery. Any subject can be a stimulus for a poem.

How to find subjects?

1. Probing your imagination and start with whatever comes into your mind. "Oh tiny bird, with humming words,"

2. Sit quietly, eyes closed and meditate on a subject. "I see, I see the world's aglow,"

3. Open your heart to one you love. "My love for you fills my heart and sweetens my soul."

4. Sit before a computer and wait for the words for any subject you desire to appear and type without hesitation." Out damn guilt, let me be free."

5. What current interest is tickling your fancy? History, science, society, politics, art. All are subjects for a poem of any length. No matter your age, no matter your time. You know and fully believe that you have the capacity to write poetry. You will not measure your words against another, nor measure your level of creativity. You will not wrestle with words or concepts. Your words will flow from you unimpeded. You are a poet.

There are many ways to initiate the flow of words. Pick up a book of poems or a novel and read until a phrase or an idea makes you pause.

Ponder what you have just read and immediately write down the first words that come into your mind. Continue to write in poetic form wherever your mind takes you. As an example, I am now reading a news article about a child who spoke harshly to a teacher and was reprimanded and sent to the principal. My mind immediately conjured up these words:

> Child, my child, you spoke in haste,
>
> And heaped upon her head, words in poor taste.
>
> Your offense was small but your tantrum was big,
>
> And you called your teacher a big fat pig.

That poem came from an actual article. It took me less than a few minutes to write. Not something I would keep. But it does illustrate that any subject can stimulate a poem.

Writing poems as a group is both fun and invigorating. You learn and share ideas and discover another method to generate a creative urge. The technique is simple. A group of friends get together, let's make it six people. The idea is to begin a joint poem. The group selects a subject and one of the participants writes the first line of a poem on a page. It is passed to the second person who responds to the idea, meaning, meter and style of writing with the second line, but written on a separate piece of paper. Only her line is passed to the next person, who continues the poem. At the end of the six-line poem or 12-line, if it is passed round twice, you have a completed poem on 12 pages, which no one has seen in its complete form. One member will then take all the papers and read the poem. Another version of this exercise is having all the participants write their lines on the same page. Everyone reads the entire poem as it is created.

You share what each has learned. Is the meaning coherent, have all the writers understood the initial and subsequent ideas giving real continuity or is the meaning scattered? This is a great way to learn how to evaluate poetry line by line.

Poetry is fun and, though usually written alone, it can also be used as a game form. It is very stimulating, perks up thinking ability. Imagine how much humor or other emotion can be aroused. You can laugh or cry or sing a poetic song but by following your deepest feelings and cleverest words you will be traveling the exciting and gratifying path of a poet in the flesh.

5

Adventures of the Soul

Nature and its unlimited manifestations touch us deeply. As in a dream, we deeply feel the interaction with trees, flowers, floating clouds and the ocean tides. A bird sings to us and we sense a messenger from God. A simple squirrel reaches for a nut and we are captured by the wildness of nature now briefly tamed and friendly. As children, we easily slipped into this mysterious and unknown dimension and came to know that world. Eventually, alas, that strange and baffling period disappeared, when we "grew out of it."

However, in our second childhood, that we can claim as older adults, we can again find the magical entrance where we can again slip back into that wonderland. When our child-selves conjure up invisible playmates, our world has given us another mysterious connection to the past and to the future. I don't think that it is strange to talk of faraway planets with Aristotle or Copernicus or discuss with Einstein our reactions to travel at the speed of light and how we experience timelessness. Except for writing these words, no one is aware that I can close my eyes and live in another world whenever I want to. You might call them daydreams. I call them adventures of the soul. So real. So mysterious.

My eyes slowly close as I sit quietly and give freedom to my creative self to go wherever it desires. I am slowly, peacefully strolling along a narrow dusty road in India. Ahead, I notice a small man sitting alone against the trunk of a Bodhi tree. As I draw near, he calls out, "Approach me and we can talk." Lured by his inviting voice and warm friendly manner I come and sit down beside him. *Yes, I think, he is the Buddha. I am in the presence of the holy man.*

I softly speak, "You have entered my thoughts many times and I have sought your wisdom in books on how to overcome my suffering. Can you help me now?"

"Yes, my son," he murmurs. "Sit closer and we will talk."

"Everyone suffers. We must recognize that our suffering is within us. It is the source of most of our ills. Until we accept this basic truth, what we call the first of our four Noble Truths, recovery is not possible. Recovery depends upon understanding the nature of your suffering is within you. The second Noble Truth is to fully grasp that we cause our own suffering. In modern terms, it comes from inner conflicts, inner negative beliefs, guilt over hate. My son, your ego directs you to activities that add to your suffering, including your greed and envy, your need to acquire material things and the excess jealousy that sometimes tears you apart. By believing in your omnipotence and lacking insight into your condition, you live in ignorance. Truth eludes you."

"But," I wanted to interject.

"One moment, my son," The Buddha smiled. "Finally, I come to the Third Noble Truth. You now focus on change, opening your eyes, discover what lies behind your suffering, your need to develop insight and overcome the conflicts that make you suffer.

"Then and only then will you follow the Fourth Noble Truth. "You will live mindfully, developing wisdom and take the path to spirituality that you will now seek."

"Buddha, I have read about noble truths and Buddhist paths and I want to live as you describe but is that necessary for me?"

"To overcome suffering and find peace and eventually spirituality, then following my advice will take you there.

"But that will take forever."

The Buddha reached out and put his hand on my shoulder. "It takes time to change. It all takes place in the mind. You will need to work to overcome the resistance that will try to thwart your efforts to change."

I listened and thought of the endless time that seemed so out of reach. Can I reach for meaning in my life each day knowing my remaining lifetime will be swallowed by this effort?

"My son," the Buddha looked intently at my perplexity. I felt his love and felt encircled by his wisdom. His final words were soft and seemed to enter my soul. "Forever is a moment or infinity. Look about you. Touch what is touchable. Seek the untouchable. Know your heart.

Open your mind. Knowledge is everywhere. Go in peace. We will meet again."

I opened my eyes, looked about and smiled.

It is time to gaze at the endlessly blue sky, look up at a passing cloud and nod to the many faces smiling down at me, hug myself and blink away the mysteriousness of my existence. As I looked about me, I remembered walking along that dusty road in India, and stopping to talk with the small man sitting quietly against the Bodhi tree.

6

Mindfulness and Your Imagination

I held out my hand as the tiny bird flitted about wondering if my hand was tempting enough to land on. Then I moved, ever so slightly, but to the tiny bird it must have appeared to be like the onrush of a tornado and the tiny bird caught the wave of air and soared away.

The bird was like a painterly palette, a blue bonnet, blue streaked wings and a white breast that seemed to heave while it flew about. Did those eyes wink at me? I laughed for I needed to watch where fantasy took over from the intensity of what I really saw. I so love to immerse myself in whatever I witness. I focused with love of the intricate and the near invisibility of objects. How easy it is to simply walk by a flower or a tree in bloom and scarcely notice these natural masterpieces. But how different when you pause and peer at the rose or daffodil or daisy and see the petals, stamen and pistil or the tiny ants scurrying down the stem. How alive they now appear. As you lovingly stare, the rose sheds its secrets. Its color vibrates and the aroma you stoop to inhale fills you with perfume.

We have meditated mindfully, concentrating on our inner self, attentive to our feelings, becoming more alive as we come to know our inner self. We recognize when we are anxious and where it derives, or what stirs us to cry or even weep. We can learn to control pain and depression and headaches. We can focus on eating and chewing our food slowly and watch as our appetite is satisfied with much less food, which can be used for dieting, if that were our purpose.

Now I want to shift mindfulness to the outside and open another path to self-awareness. It is meditation in motion, mindfulness in action. Let's take a walk together. Outside I briefly stop on a sidewalk just outside my home and take a deep breath. The air is clean, fresh, and rushes into my lungs. The quietness is startling, I imagine that all sound has ceased.

I begin to walk centering my mind on the feelings in my body as I stretch out my legs and sense the muscles contracting and expanding. I now stretch my arms to the side and upwards and increase my speed heading toward a clump of trees that I know so well. I gaze and extend my mind toward the sculptural trees that watch me pass. I nod hello to the giraffe and the monkey with the long tail, old friends from previous walks. How well I know those trees, I thought. Every branch tells a story.

Today a crow sat alone on a long, crooked branch protruding like a weaving snake from a majestic oak. I stopped and waved hello, but was totally ignored until I stepped closer to the tree and the crow flew to the ground alighting on the grass nearby but now watching me warily. I believe I caught her eye and in an inner silent voice introduced myself and told her how beautiful she is. The crow moved closer and we looked knowingly at each other. I stood still until, I believe, the crow smiled at me just before she flew off.

Is this mindfulness, you might ask? Yes, I believe so. The interaction with the animal branches and the beautiful crow would have only occurred with my complete focus and the mindful use of my imagination. What is important is to open your mind to another sphere of energy and creativity that comes with your concentration upon anything you experience. You can look at a stone and see odd shapes, changes in color, perhaps figures. Change your view and look upward and notice the clouds cavorting overhead, faces, figures, staring down at you. Look at people walking near you and imagine them as a famous person, or see a small Maltese or beagle or a retriever respond to your unspoken message to them as you pass by. They always acknowledge your greeting.

After our extended walk, I encourage you to follow your own path to give new meaning to your use of mindfulness. Take it with you outside or into libraries or out to dinner and into a theater. Watch dance, skating and sports. Watch the finesse and beauty of an NBA basketball player leap and throw and see how their skills unfold. The same extends to golfers, including yourself. There is no limit to where you can bring such focus to enhance your life. You are now on the verge of new adventures of the mind.

7
The Heart of Spirituality

What does it mean to feel the aliveness of spirit? As we grow older and our lives become simpler, our material existence seems to wither away replaced by one of feeling and a wish for simplicity. We strive to touch our inner soul. Our need to acquire objects diminishes as our inner selves clamor for moral and emotional sustenance. Can these changes be part of what we feel as spirituality?

Many religious leaders and philosophers speak of spirituality arising from love and even equate love and spirituality. Is it the love of God that awakens spirituality or the love of humanity or nature? Does it matter where spirituality comes from? What do we feel when we know we are spiritual? Does spirituality come from a deep sense of peacefulness and kindness toward others with whom we share our essential being? Does it come from being religious? In recent centuries, spirituality has been separated from organized religions. Nevertheless, many people believe that their religious beliefs and the hope of going to Heaven foster their spirituality.

For those who believe that spirituality exists independent of religion and may be more akin to an inherited instinct that comes with birth there are many other avenues of belief in spirituality. Many believe that giving to others and sharing feelings and possessions are evidence of spirituality. Those who are deeply immersed in nature and feel intertwined with nature's beauty feel spiritual and deeply fulfilled. Those who love and live in the wonders of music often believe that music is a special link to God and their spirituality is ingrained with God's love of music. Those who feel spiritual and not religious believe that the underlying feeling of all believers in their own spirituality, whatever its basis, is love.

Is there a theme here? Excluding those who accept that it is given by God, we are left with the deeply believed equation of spirituality and love. Thus love of nature, music, animals, birds, poetry, as well as love of people, can fill one with feelings of spirituality. Many of those filled with love are immersed in deep connections to many elements of life. Loving nature almost always leads to loving music and animals. Once embraced by genuine spirituality people live in a state of near perpetual peace and happiness.

Many people, however, question their belief in spirituality. What are they lacking? Many ask how they would know if they were spiritual? "What kind of feeling would I have other than just assuming I am spiritual?" Perhaps we may recognize that there are unique words and feelings, even something beyond words and feelings, a quality of being that is unique for spirituality. In a sense, it fills the same kind of emotion that comes with listening to music. It is there; you know it, but no words suffice to describe it. Perhaps we may liken it to a special kind of poetry that kindles an inner flame of love and well-being. The poem reaches deep within and far-reaching without.

For many, peacefulness reached through meditation and mindfulness is felt as being spiritual. Whatever is the basis of spirituality, it offers us a life where we touch others with warmth and unbridled love that changes our world even as we change the world of others.

I would like to suggest that all seekers of spirituality follow the path of those who live by the depth of their love. Free yourself of barriers to loving; reach out and clasp to your heart those you love. There should be no struggle to love. There is an internal spring of desire to connect with others. Love appears even in stillness and periods of quietude. There is no struggle. Instead, a lifetime of spiritual growth awaits you. Openness to a spiritual life is natural and desired. It follows the path to give love and to be loved.

Love brings you into the world of spirit and the desire to share your life with the world that surrounds you. Make spirituality a gift to yourself. Increase ways to give to others as you continue to offer kindness and love to those you touch. Your spirituality will deepen as your bounty reflects back to you and you attain a life of peace and joy. By spreading your personal happiness, you become linked to the world that surrounds you. I know of no better way to bring fulfillment and a sense of inner joy than becoming immersed in your spirituality and reacting to the world with your new vision. Your life will be one where your love of life, nature and God fulfills you. You will live in a world of tranquility.

8

An Easy to Use Effective Diet Program

In this day and age with new diets sprouting up frequently, all claiming to work wonders to lose weight and maintain weight control, dieters linger between jumping for joy and sliding into despair and often join the yo-yo group of dieters who gain and lose weight on a regular basis. Unless you have already latched onto a diet program that appears to be working for you, what do you do? Each diet tends to claim major adherents, often celebrities, giving you health advice and promises, sometimes promoting programs that will also cure many ailments and guaranteeing that you will lose weight. Since almost all diets work initially, they gain adherents for a time. Some also work well by having dieters attend weekly meetings or scheduled visits to a doctor or clinic or eating prescribed food.

For those seeking a healthy, easy to use and effective diet I would like to introduce a new diet program that can be used for maintaining weight or to lose weight. The basic foods should be based on low fat (25-30%), protein (15%), carbohydrates (50-60%), emphasizing whole grains, fish and lean meat, vegetables and fruits. Check the Mediterranean Diet.

The program comprises five key elements.

1. WATER

Useful for both losing weight and maintaining a stable weight.

Timing: On awakening, drink one glass of water. Before each meal drink one glass and during the meal drink another glass.

Before each snack, drink ½ glass of water.

Water helps fill the stomach and reduces your craving when used with food. You feel full more quickly and eat less.

2. THE BATHROOM SCALE.

Develop a positive relationship with your scale and become friends with it. Most people avoid daily weighing fearing it will show that they have gained weight. However, that information is necessary to know for this new diet. Weigh yourself each morning before eating or drinking anything; same way, same time. That's how you'll know if you've gained any weight, day by day. If you have, thank the scale for the info. Then you'll know what you have to do. **Use the one-day water diet.**

3. THE ONE-DAY WATER DIET

The one-day water diet is useful for those on a diet to lose weight and for those who are trying to maintain their weight. This simple water diet helps dieters overcome despair and guilt caused by the one day overeating that they believe is permanent.

For each pound you have gained from the previous day, drink an extra 1 ½ glasses of water. Make certain this is **extra** water, added to the usual 8 or 10 glasses you normally drink. Coffee and tea can count as water.

How does this work? Most weight gained in a single day is due to water retention. If you splurged the day before, it would only take an additional 800-1200 calories with the salt component in the food to increase your weight a couple of pounds. More added calories, more added weight.

Why does this occur? Most foods contain salt. The body retains water to dilute that salt, which gives you a temporary weight increase. The extra water you drink from the one-day water diet is quickly excreted by the kidney, usually in the next 24 hours, taking the added salt with it. By the next day or two you are back to your normal pre-splurge weight. If you're concerned about the extra weight from the added calories, decrease your food intake by about 400 calories for two days.

4. TAKING OFF THE REAL, NON-WATER POUNDS.

To lose weight by dieting, reduce your daily calories by 400 to 500 (usually 20% of your normal intake). It takes 3300 calories to lose one pound of body tissue. You will lose a minimum of four pounds a month.

Just cut back on your normal foods. Losing weight should be easy now that you know water will assist you.

5. THE STABILIZATION PERIOD

Diet for only one month at a time; then stop the next month and maintain weight. That is the **stabilization** period. Each alternate month should bring you closer to your desired goal. It should be relatively easy because the weight you've lost in the month you dieted is so little. During the stabilization periods you will become a master at weight control. Once you have reached your ideal weight it will be easy to stop dieting and to not be afraid of regaining your weight. Alternate monthly dieting will prevent or impede any decrease in your metabolic rate, the usual reason why most dieters regain their lost weight when they resume a normal diet.

This is a simple formula for weight control. Try it. It works. If you have a relapse, don't worry; you can immediately resume your diet and get back on track.

9

The Complexity of Healthful Eating

Love the superfoods, such as spinach, kale, broccoli, carrots, sweet potatoes, wild salmon, butternut squash and enjoy the delicious berries, watermelon and mangoes. And indulge occasionally in delectable desserts. Of course, make those all-encompassing smoothies that feed your health and delight. Most of these healthy meals are made at home, although restaurants are serving increasingly healthy, low calorie, low fat meals for discriminating diners.

My purpose is to keep you healthy and not to interfere with your being able to enjoy your meals, and especially the fun of eating out. Let's get down to what I'm leading up to. It's being aware of the harmful ingredients that are part of the usual daily intake of food that all of us eat. There are many substances where individuals have little control over their presence and use. They include herbicides to control weeds and grasses and various pesticides, such as insecticides to eradicate insects and bugs, rodenticides to destroy rodents as rats and gophers, and fungicides to eliminate plant molds that cause various illnesses.

There are air borne poisons that arise as by-products in certain manufacturing processes. The smoke from coal power plants containing coal dust and particulate matter is especially dangerous. Although there are still over 300 coal power plants in the USA, they are gradually closing. Along with the manufacture of oil, coal power plants produce most of the airborne mercury that eventually falls in the oceans and has caused the rise of mercury in fish, making many dangerous to eat. High levels of mercury is a threat to in utero development and in young children. Toxic levels can negatively affect the nervous system, especially the brain and the immune system.

Arsenic, a known carcinogen, which occurs naturally throughout the world in soil, water and air is present in many foods especially grains, fruit juices, vegetables and fish. Recently it has been determined that arsenic in rice, especially brown rice, and in some drinking water is increasing. Although we hear reassurance that the arsenic is below danger levels, many doubts have risen. When coupled with mercury its danger multiplies.

And what of the thousands of new substances developed each year that contaminate our food and medical systems. Many turn out to be potentially dangerous and only removed from circulation after years of use. Despite the FDA and other regulatory agencies and organizations overseeing our health these dangers continue. Another example is the prescription of multiple drugs for a single patient by doctors, often unaware of the interaction of the prescribed drugs or that his patient is using drugs from another physician.

The specific foods we eat can also negatively influence our health and longevity. Namely, the specific foods that each of us selects for our daily diet. The choices we make in just one day of eating are so varied and so personal that it is difficult to comment on different diets and what creates the basis for a healthy life. The diets that we follow are quite variable as you can see in the number that I list. Naming just a few gives you an idea of why your food intake may vary. Weight Watchers, Jenny Craig, Atkins, Ornish, Nutrisystem, high fat, low fat, etc. All the current diets can't be equally healthy. How does one know? As a solo subject we can't go on a double blind diet, where, for example, we eat a low or a high fat diet. We do one or the other.

However, each person does make selections, either by conscious choice or by chance and hit or miss, depending on what is available. They involve specific foods that you individually select. The variety is often made by taste, what feels satisfying, filling up, part of a cultural or social norm or just following an impulse or a psychological craving.

What constitutes a healthy diet and ways to control weight and what constitutes a reasonable approach to losing weight. In this case, the government guidelines have it right. The following limits are reasonable and simple to follow. Carbohydrates-50-55%, fat- up to 30%, preferably limited to 25% with a maximal input of saturated fats of 10% and preferably eating primarily polyunsaturated and monounsaturated fatty acids and protein of 15% (to 20%). All other diets are fads or emphasizing individual ingredients and generally don't work for long.

Weight control and losing weight are strictly a matter of diminishing your daily intake of food by 25% of your normal calorie intake. Do it gradually and slowly. Every other month stop dieting and adjust to your small monthly loss. This works.

Healthy diets avoid or minimize processed foods, especially meats, foods with high salt levels, high added sugar, saturated fats, trans fats and fried foods. Bleached grains, such as white bread, fancy high calorie coffees, high calorie desserts and frequent nibbling, snacking and raiding the refrigerator should be avoided. Heed your impulses, think though your lifestyle, place personal health at the head of your list. It's a winning position.

10

Laughter

---

*"There is nothing in the world so irresistibly
contagious as laughter and good humor."*

— Charles Dickens, *A Christmas Carol*

Ho Ho Ho fills the air and we all look up and see the reindeer bounding along pulling a huge sled and a man in red pajamas. So you think it is Christmas. I tell you it is everyday. Those reindeer slide to a halt and saunter over for a pat on the nose and a little treat, lick my nose and whisper, "let's go for a ride." Wild, untamed, with the wind swirling around, they skim over the tops of trees. I love it. Every day, I soar into the sky. You can too. Smile and wish and you're on your way. Oh, do I love my imagination.

Laugh, my friends. It all starts with humor, and wide-eyes childish glee, total innocence. But laugh, laugh, laugh. From day one to the end of time, laugh. You grow and laugh and grow stronger. You raise kids and you better laugh. You already know that the kids will laugh at you, if you falter. Exercise your jaw, up, down, left, right, oblique, in and out, your stomach puffing away until you're rolling across the room, may as well bounce on the way, that can really be funny.

You'll never notice that you have become older for "With mirth and laughter let old wrinkles come," said our guru **William Shakespeare, in** *The Merchant of Venice*. You only need to laugh. Age disappears. Life bolsters you along. Remember the day you reached out fruitlessly to catch a butterfly and only managed to snare a moth that just happened to land on your nose. Now if you don't laugh at that coincidence, when you let the moth go free, you're beyond getting old. If so, my ancient friend, you do need help. Here I'll push you across the floor and get you started.

Sorry for the interruption but I was rolling again on the floor laughing my head off. Do you mind waiting one more moment while I go to find it, my head that is, since I almost started to write again without my head. Imagine writing without my head on. Hmm, I'm trying to imagine if that is funny or just pathetic.

OK, you get my drift. If you're not laughing at this crazy article by now then you do need an article to advise you to laugh.

Enough for you need to know that humor and laughing are an undeniable path to good health, maintaining your intelligence, preventing dementia and not going crazy trying to find a parking place at Whole Foods. Be bold, push forward, live on your own terms and make your own conditions. No conformity for you. Kick adversity down the road and wave goodbye. Dance and skip. Walking's for kids unless heading for Kilimanjaro.

My case is made: laughter is strong medicine. Taken daily it enhances healthy physical and emotional changes in the body. Laughter strengthens your immune system by decreasing stress hormones and increasing immune cells and infection-fighting antibodies, thus improving your resistance to disease.

It improves mood and lessens pain. Humor lightens your burdens, inspires hope, connects you to others, and keeps you grounded, focused, and alert. It also helps you release anger and forgive sooner.

Laughter protects the heart. It improves the function of blood vessels and increases blood flow, which can help prevent a heart attack and other cardiovascular problems.

With so much power to heal and renew, the ability to laugh easily and frequently is a tremendous resource for surmounting problems, enhancing your relationships, and supporting both physical and emotional health. Best of all, this priceless medicine is fun, free, and easy to use.

As children, we used to laugh hundreds of times a day, but as adults, life tends to be more serious and laughter more infrequent. But by seeking out more opportunities for humor and laughter, you can improve your emotional health, strengthen your relationships. You will find greater happiness—and even add years to your life.

Laughter lightens anger's heavy load. Nothing diffuses anger and conflict faster than a shared laugh. Looking at the funny side can put problems into perspective and enable you to move on from confrontations without holding onto bitterness or resentment. What a great way to enhance building and maintaining friendships.

Laughter may even help you to live longer. A study in Norway found that people with a strong sense of humor outlived those who don't laugh as much. The difference was particularly notable for those battling cancer. In other words, believe in life, endless life and not assume that cancer or any other illness will take your life. Don't dwell on life ending. Until your last breath believe in your aliveness.

11
Balance: Preventing Falling

Falling is not an option in living. Many falls are dangerous and even deadly. As we get older the danger increases. Poor balance is the enemy. Poor balance must end.

Balance depends upon a number of interrelated physical and mental elements that change as the body ages and weakens. Any or all can be contributing to your balance difficulties.

1. Muscle weakness, especially lower extremities.

2. Ear problems as vestibular and semicircular disorders, brain changes in temporal, cerebellar and motor cortex.

3. Vascular brain changes, small strokes.

4. Side effects of certain medications, as antihistamines, sedatives, and blood pressure drugs.

5. Alcohol, pot, other psychedelic drugs.

6. Parkinson's Disease.

7. Low Blood pressure. lightheaded.

8. Neurological disorders, such as peripheral neuropathology, loss of sensation in feet. Vertigo. Headaches, especially migraine.

9. Lack of sleep, tired, inattentive, not focused.

Whatever the cause or causes of your balance difficulties and tendencies to fall, you can, without doubt, lessen the probability of falling. When we realize that most falls occur in the house, under normal living conditions, then it behooves us to look around our home and remove any obstacles and dangerous objects that are lying around. That includes unattached rugs, extension cords, runners, easily moved boxes, loose clothing and paper scattered on the floor, fallen books, toys, games, water and grease in the kitchen and bathrooms. Unless you have dutifully acted on these self-protective actions, then you need to immediately look around and safety-proof your home.

Don't stand on chairs or anything more than a low safety stool made for the purpose of reaching for needed objects, as food, in cabinets. Better put everything on lower shelves and have a neighbor, or a taller person reach for higher objects. Do not go around the house barefooted or wearing smooth stockings. Always wear well-fitted shoes with rubber soles and low heels. Loose sandals can cause tripping. Don't wear dresses that drag on the floor or wide pants that stretch to the floor.

Since falling is the number one cause of injury to seniors, with one senior in three falling each year and many breaking bones that often leads to death, it can't be overemphasized to take all the precautions possible. When you walk, take smaller steps, stop when you intend to change directions or look at an object or scene. **Stop first and turn your entire body.** This is one of the more important changes most walkers need to make.

When climbing stairs hold on the banister. Only hold packages in one hand so that one arm is always free for the banister. At home when you rise from a chair, stop before stepping away from it. Learn to always stop before making new moves. Move slowly. Make this a habit. This includes rising from dinner, the sofa in front of a coffee table, an outdoor chair. Two essential habits to cultivate are STOPPING before moving and SLOWING UP.

Cultivate the belief that you can control your body if you do fall. Is this possible? YES. Minor shifts in your body, even as you have lost balance, can mean the difference between a broken bone or back and having soft tissue injury, if any injury at all. Here are the essential elements to know to avoid injury in falling.

1. Learn how to relax your body mentally. Meditate while sitting in a chair and imagine seeing your entire body go limp. Visualize your body in various states of being; standing, sitting, lurching forward and backward, all while extremely relaxed.

2. The second imagery is seeing yourself walking and falling forward. At the same time you strongly feel your body relax even as you know you are about to hit the ground. Now imagine, as you are falling, that you turn your body in mid air and fall on your side, on soft tissue and by not landing on your hands, you are avoiding breaking your wrists.

3. Imagine you are falling backward. Now tuck your head forward and hold down in your hands to avoid hitting your head on the ground. As you become more adept with this imagery, follow by turning your body and landing on your side.

This imagery is for the mind. **Don't practice these exercises.**

At a gym as well as at your home practice a variety of balance exercises, such as standing on one foot, doing heel to toe walking and doing squats for strong legs.

There are many books available that present exercises for balance. In addition, it is prudent to enlist the support or assistance of a trainer to help you set up an exercise program which you can execute alone.

Avoiding falling is of such importance that you cannot overdo attempting to revise and improve your ability to find and live with better balance. Your self-esteem will soar as your balance improves.

12

The Challenge of Control: Do Not Fall

DO NOT FALL: Must be a mantra, so important is this subject that a second article was mandated. Read on:

"I feel so tired of being careful of not falling," a dear friend said to me recently. Three days later she tripped, fell forward and injured herself. The impetus for this article immediately came into my mind. Everyone, especially the aging population, must develop a new mindset, a new sense of awareness about their body movements, activities, how they move. You must strive to gain conscious and consistent control over your actions. You owe it to your body.

No more can anyone take for granted that their normal instinctive control over body movements is sufficient to prevent falling. We reflect back when younger and remember running, doing daredevil movements, dashing about without the need to watch every step. No more. We all need a new consciousness. We must do everything to avoid falling

Falls are a major cause of injury and hospitalization and ultimately a major factor in becoming ill and even dying. Hospitals are aware of the danger of falling for any patient, no matter what brought them into the hospital or to the Emergency Room. In hospitals there are signs in every room and in hallways warning of the dangers of falling. "Call don't fall." "Call for help."

So, what do we do? We change our habits of walking, moving, and reacting to our environment. We are going to establish a new, powerful mindset energized by an incredibly positive attitude of not falling. Is that possible? Absolutely. **We again will use mindfulness, concentrating on our actions and reflexes to initiate change.** We will become mindful of all dangers that may contribute to falling. We will become more conscious of our feelings, knowing when we feel negative, that is less watchful of our actions. Being negative reduces our overall concentration. Reducing negativity becomes imperative. Simultaneously we increase the awareness of those actions that can contribute to falling. To avoid falling the concentration must be continuous. Falling is anathema. It is forbidden. Strong words. How can you forbid a mental or physical action? You must believe that you can master this change in attitude. And you can.

Areas for special alertness.

1. When you walk, walk with your eyes looking ahead and switching back and forth to also looking at the ground in front of you.

2. There are dangers on every walk: such as broken pavement areas, roots causing unevenness on sidewalk, acorns, slippery leaves, dog poo.

3. Speaking on a cell phone can reduce your attention to other dangers noted.

4. As you walk and attempt to look at a passing object, such as a bird, flower or tree you are jeopardizing your ability to keep upright. If want to look at something stop and turn your whole body and then focus on the object. In essence, **you pause, look and enjoy. Remember turning**, even after you have stopped walking, can cause you to fall.

5. Leaning forward or sideways can lead to falling as you lose balance and can't stop your momentum. It can occur getting out of a car, going through doorways, going up and down staircases, picking up your mail. Learn your point of vulnerability. Know when you can't stop your momentum.

6. Be careful on stairs, especially starting to descend and coming to the bottom stair, which may be more or less steep than anticipated which can jar your back or cause you to fall.

7. The same walking on the sidewalk where the heights of the sidewalk may be deceptive. If you are not looking you take an unexpected action. If uncertain, hold on to something and look. Don't hesitate to have someone help you.

8. It takes little to fall off a ladder. Avoid stepping stools. Let others reach up. No embarrassment in needing help. Keep in mind that it is not easy to break old habits. Going up and down steps

used to be automatic. Now you need a railing or someone's arm to navigate steps.

9. Getting out of bed, many fall. Get rid of anything you might trip on: slippers, rugs, clothes, anything. Take up all small area rugs. Likewise, the bathroom, the shower or tub are areas of potential danger. Most falls occur in homes. I encourage a new way of thinking. Everything you do is scrutinized to determine what contributes to not falling.

There are two little mental tricks I recommend. Sit quietly, eyes closed. Visualize being in an area with multiple obstacles and you run into all of them. You see the immense danger of falling. You become super focused and a bright light appears in your mind and steers you through the obstacles. You convincingly say that you will always be extremely careful and avoid all obstacles. You repeat, "I will be extremely alert to whatever I do. I will not fall. I will not fall." Do this exercise daily until you have gained the control you desire.

Become confident in your ability to maintain active control over all body movements.

13

Reckoning with Our Fears

The number of different fears that can appear as aging continues strongly influences the degree of satisfaction we achieve in our final years. New and old concerns about real and unreal illnesses take hold of our imagination and a deepening fear of illness, even fatal illness, envelopes our minds. Fear of our own impending death frequently takes hold of us initiated by the loss of a spouse, a family member or a loved friend. Dying may become a dominant fear. The need to overcome these fears is necessary to find the way back to a happy life. Death is inevitable, but fear is not.

The pall on activities that were shared with a friend now gone may be hard to lift. Following a period of mourning of varying length, we need to remain with good memories of a life now gone. To reiterate, we must be careful not to turn the death of a loved one into an increasing fear of our own death. As we get older, it is important to understand that our primary need is to rejoice in the life that each of us has.

When you first experience a normal temporary loss of memory of a name or word, the fear of dementia rears its head. A friend trips and breaks a bone and you become extra careful in walking and climbing and may even curtail your physical freedom. At times, a fear of falling makes people less secure as they begin to overreact to situations that now seem daunting and even dangerous.

A near car accident may give rise to an incipient fear of driving. Yet even when driving skills have obviously lessened, the idea of giving up driving to some older people spells loss of freedom. Becoming a prisoner of one's home is frightening and can lead to depression. It may take time to develop a new point of view that not driving can lead to a different kind of freedom. The availability of drivers, buses, Uber, Lyft and saving the cost of owning a car, provide advantages. All is a matter of perspective.

Fears also spread to activities outside the body. Political instability that may appear to endanger health insurance and long-term care creates insecurity and concern with longevity and being unable to get the medical care needed. Global warming and the lack of climate control have awakened long-term fears of frightening storms, excessive heat, rising sea levels and the prospect of eroding sea coasts and beaches despite that the true impact lies in the future. Closer to our lives is the increasing number of fires sweeping our state. Many are deeply concerned for the world we are leaving our children and grandchildren. Predictions of daily temperatures in the 100s, and the flooding of the large cities of the country, accented by superstorms are appearing more regularly but are still ignored and even denied by our government. This fear is still in its early stage but will mount in the coming years.

With growing weakness coupled to problems with balance, vision, hearing impairment and various chronic illnesses worsening for many seniors, fears of not living freely intensify. The dread of being alone with increasing loneliness often enters the life of older people. Loneliness is often felt as a defeat of the liveliness and self-direction they have maintained much of their lives. With the loss of a spouse, friends, and good health, such loneliness is accentuated, often accompanied by fear of isolation. Unless a person is capable of making a life as a loner and has a few friends or family to help through difficult and needy periods, the resulting loneliness may result in depression, which may require treatment.

Facing our many fears is the task we now undertake. We need solutions to overcome our fears, especially those that seem to threaten our health and our lives. Now is the time to call upon all our resources that we have learned and put them to use. They include:

1. The use of mental imagery and affirmations emphasizing special use of end-state imagery

2. Finding spiritual outlets

3. Seeking new friends, activities and venues, adding special events to your life

4. Seeking medical and other forms of therapy, if needed for any lingering illness

5. Opening creative paths for fulfillment, especially in the areas of art, crafts and writing

6. Learning a musical instrument. Join a chorus. Sing

7. Stimulating your minds through book clubs, returning to school, and the Learning Company's Great Courses

Most important is actively redirecting yourself into a new and meaningful lifestyle. The benefits will be enormous. And it will all come from your own efforts and desires. You can create a new and fulfilling life. You must believe in your ability to change and to enjoy each day you are alive.

14

Understanding Heart Disease

It's time to have a heart to heart talk about, you guessed it, the heart and demolish once and for all your fears of having a heart attack. Understandably, with Heart Disease being the number one health killer in the US and the world, it is a cause of much of the fear that grips older people. However, most heart attacks are not fatal but depend on what artery is involved, whether there is a blood clot or a rupture of the artery causing the heart attack, and the immediate treatment given when the symptoms occur.

The primary type of attack is a myocardial infarction caused by a blockage of blood flow to the heart usually caused by a clot from a ruptured plague on the lining of a coronary artery, hence the name coronary artery disease (CAD). The area of the heart supplied by that artery quickly becomes non-functional.

Cardiac arrest, the most dangerous form of heart attack, tends to elicit the greatest fear since it can quickly lead to death. Although usually caused by a heart attack that blocks blood flow to the heart, the heart's electrical system giving rise most commonly to an irregular, rapidly beating heart rhythm known as atrial fibrillation or Afib, which causes the heart's blood output to diminish. is often responsible for cardiac arrest.

The far more dangerous ventricular fibrillation can also occur, which usually prevents adequate blood flow to the heart and brain leading to loss of consciousness. Less frequently, the electrical system stops the heart's ventricle from beating completely. Other causes of cardiac arrest are due to heart failure, lung clots, mineral imbalances, such as potassium and drug overdoses. Using CPR, hands only, until the medics arrive, can be life saving.

Chewing and swallowing a full-sized, non-enteric aspirin tablet when you believe you have had a heart attack to diminish the effect of the clot and reduce additional damage is vitally important. Immediately following taking the aspirin, dial 911 and contact emergency help. Hospital treatment is directed at clot removal and use of anticoagulants to dissolve clots and forestall additional clotting.

Knowledge is the key to overcome these fears. Most of us know the common symptoms of a heart attack but repetition may be useful. 1. Chest pain, may appear as squeezing, pressure, sometimes misdiagnosed as indigestion. 2. Shortness of breath. 3. Pain or aching that radiates to an arm, usually the left one, to the jaw, shoulder, back and stomach. 4. Nausea with or without vomiting. 5. Dizziness, feeling faint. 6. Sudden fatigue. 7. Cold and clammy skin. 8. Sweating. 9. Many heart attacks occur without the person's awareness.

Can we prevent or diminish the probability of having a heart attack? My objective is to eliminate having a heart attack in the first place. Is it possible to prevent one, even in people who are genetically predisposed to the condition? No guarantees but over many long-term studies there is considerable evidence that not smoking, maintaining a proper diet and adequate exercise, reduction of emotional stress, avoiding illegal drugs and being careful about drug interactions will help you avoid having a heart attack. Discuss with your doctor and your pharmacist potential dangers of mixing drugs.

Diet and exercise that influence heart health are the two areas that can be changed and improved. First diet: Reduce fat intake and cholesterol-laden foods. Keep total cholesterol under 200 mg/dl. Any level above 240 mg/dl. Is too high. Try to reduce without taking statin drugs, if possible. Lose weight, if you are heavy.

Exercise: General body exercising and stretching at least every other day and walking for 30 minutes, five or more times a week, are the most important activities for your heart. Exercise also helps general health, helps keep you younger longer, keeps your mind sharper and reduces dementia.

Hypertension, a major cause of cardiac disease and heart failure, tends to increase as people age. The new guidelines indicate that those over 65 need to keep their pressure under 120/80. However, many cardiologists believe that people over 70 need more leeway and can live safely with a systolic (upper number) BP of 130 mm or 140 mm and a diastolic of up to 90 mm. BP can be reduced by limiting salt intake to 1500 mg./ daily with a top of 1800 mg. Diets rich in fruits, vegetables and fiber tend to reduce BP.

Other ways to avoid heart disease include: maintaining good general health, getting adequate sleep, practicing daily mindful meditation, reducing stress, having periods of peaceful relaxation and engaging in pleasurable activities.

There are no miracles to prevent heart attacks but innumerable studies have shown that reducing the factors that contribute to heart disease will lengthen your life. You want to be free of anxiety about your heart, take proper care of your health, seek medical treatment when needed and maintain personal health indefinitely.

15

The Prevention of Heart Disease

A quiet voice inside my head whispered repeatedly, "I'm doing everything to stop cancer, but I'm really worried about my heart. I even get scared when I feel it beating wildly, when I exercise. Isn't that supposed to be good for the heart?" Yes and no. What kind of shape are you in? Can you run marathons? Can you walk a brisk mile? Our initial assessment requires you to take a good and honest look at your mental and physical self. The objective is to know yourself and then read on and learn more about keeping your heart and yourself healthy.

Are you highly attentive to what you eat, the level and kinds of exercise, the adequacy of your sleep and rest? Do you control your anger, deal with your fears? Do you make sharing, friendship and love dominant parts of your emotional makeup? Are you recovering from a recent heart attack and understand the proper programs and lifestyle you should adopt? I hope to address many of these issues in the article that follows.

Moderation is the key for heart health. It depends on a variety of things, including age, physical well-being, genetic factors, body weight. Use judgment. Avoid excessiveness.

Try to get a better understanding for the degree of danger you have for heart failure or a heart attack. Check with your doctor. If your potential is high you should consider the following tests.

Coronary artery calcium (CAC) scores may indicate the potential for a person having a heart attack and predict a person's chance of dying over the following 10 to 15 years. If your score is high there is greater urgency to follow stringent healthy heart programs.

Chronic inflammation occurs in the body from the result of longtime exposure to toxins and poisons, such as smoke from cigarettes, lead from paint, pesticides and heavy smog. They play a role in the development of atherosclerosis leading to plagues in the arteries, which eventually may rupture forming a clot, blocking blood flow and causing a heart attack.

The level of inflammation can be established by testing for CRP (C-reactive protein), Many doctors still do not test for CRP since there has been no established drug to treat the inflammation, but new drugs are currently being tested that appear to be beneficial.

In addition to the blood tests various symptoms and changes in behavior, stamina and consciousness may be early clues to increasing vulnerability. Sudden or growing weakness may be due to impending heart disease. Chest pain or pain down the left arm and sometimes the right arm, back, jaw and shoulder, especially on exertion are frequent symptoms of heart disease. Angina pectoris, a sharp pain in chest, is a typical symptoms of heart trouble. Keep in mind that heart attacks can occur without any pain.

Only half the people recognize when a heart attack has occurred, Some think it was an attack of indigestion or muscle pain. People with a high threshold for pain or with diabetes when neuropathy has dulled the sensation of pain are among those who often remain unaware. It is important to have medical evaluation if you have suggestive symptoms of an actual heart attack. Treatment, and changes in behavior and lifestyle may be indicated. An EKG is diagnostic.

What to do if your health background, eating habits, weight, poor exercise habits, age and genetics point to the likelihood of impending heart trouble? Simple! Change your lifestyle. Not difficult to do and considering the benefits a no-brainer. Exercise heads the list. Walk, attend the fitness center, use a personal trainer. Diet. Stop gaining weight. If heavy, try to lose weight. Stop using processed food. Eat fewer fatty foods and sweet desserts. Learn to relax using mindfulness meditation. Stop smoking, if you still do. No heavy drinking. Adequate rest and sleep. Develop friendships if you live alone and are lonely. Exercise your mind with creative efforts and joining clubs.

Now I would like to leave you with several effective mental exercises that can be used by all interested in improving their heart and general health.

Sit quietly, close your eyes, take a deep breath and let your body completely relax. Imagine a deep healing light entering your body from above and slowly and progressively move down and warming and healing your entire body. Note as it caresses your brain and heart, enters your lungs and kidneys, pancreas and bathes your liver, spleen and intestinal track. Your entire nervous system tingles with new energy and your muscles ripple with potential action.

End the exercise with the simple thought. "Every day, I find new and increasing vigor and wellbeing throughout my mind and body."

Kudos to your new sense of aliveness and growing health. You will live a very hearty life.

16

The Prevention of Cancer

Today we gather our forces to combat the insidious and intrusive enemy, cancer. Cancer confronts us in many guises. They don't hesitate to attack when they have an opening. They come in forms initially not recognized though clues are often visible, such as changes in skin moles. They incorporate multiple weapons from genetic vulnerability to the outpouring of certain hormones to the tiniest viruses. They show no hesitation to confront our normal defenses and fight T cells for control of our body. They seek ever inventive ways to overcome obstacles to break through our defenses. How do we fight them? What forces can we erect to stop them in their tracks, turn them back, defeat them.

The overall approach is complex and may appear difficult to accomplish. We must mobilize greater forces when cancer becomes overbearing. They are unrelenting and we must become equally unrelenting. We must discover all methods to forestall their power and become more invincible. We need to put up walls to make us impenetrable and find ways to combat them once they have gained a foothold inside our bodies.

We need to recognize that all parts of our bodies are exposed to cancer attacks. No area remains free of cancer assaults. How do we erect what might be considered a major global protector against all cancer? Certainly, we want to continue to fight all specific cancers. Initially, always be alert to any external dangers, such as asbestos, lead in old paint, getting close to and breathing in pesticides used to control weeds and ward off pests from flowers and trees.

Now, if we could find ways to strengthen the bodies' resistance to all cancers that would be of inestimable value for health and longevity. How would we do that?

We need to make it more difficult for cancer to find entrance into the body. I doubt that putting up a sign on our body that says "Cancer stay away" would influence it but anything that we do to make it more difficult for them to find entrance would simulate that sign. NO crystal ball needed here. **Four things** come to mind immediately. The first is **diet**, the second is **exercise**, the third is using **mental techniques** designed to fight cancer in its various forms and the fourth is adequate **rest and sleep**.

The easiest improvement to make with known benefits is **diet changes**. Not only does it improve body health but gives you more energy, helps you lose weight, if desired. First, establish a plant-based diet with fish and poultry added. Minimize the use of meat. Nuts, several ounces a day add to energy and health. Drink adequate water, eight glasses a day, which can include tea, limited coffee and up to a half glass of wine at dinner. Fruit, several daily and, at times, don't hesitate to indulge in one of your favorite desserts. Sounds delicious, as well as mentally healthful. Keep control of size.

Next is **exercise**. You already know my favorite. Walk daily, fifteen minutes to an hour. Other aerobic exercises are equally beneficial, as using a tread mill, elliptical glider, or a stationary bicycle. Dancing, yoga classes, tai chi, swimming, tennis, pickle ball, ping pong, volley ball and various other aerobic classes add to the mix.

Mental techniques include meditation, practicing mindfulness, use of mental imagery and setting up exercises that strengthen the body's ability to ward off diseases of all types and especially directed to fighting the known causes of cancer. A simple **mental imagery exercise** while sitting quietly with eyes closed is imagining an army of T cells gathering in every blood vessel, and sweeping the body clean of all disease. Repeat several times. **Meditation**, usually one or two periods of about 15 minutes daily is enjoyed by those using it. **Mindfulness** and its power in helping you focus on your inner conflicts helps reduce harmful stress. Finally, maintaining a strong, **unwavering belief** in continuing to have good health and taking a very positive position of your view in fighting cancer.

Your positive beliefs should include setting up barriers to all illnesses, including the common cold. By repeating the affirmations daily and believing in your words you slowly create an internal change in your physical self. The mind can change the body as we have seen in the use of mental imagery used by athletes, actors and people in general.

Rest and sleep are essential. Seven to eight hours of sleep a night is a reasonable goal, perhaps nine hours is useful for some elderly, who may need more sleep. Periods of rest, including naps, whether in half hour bundles several times a day or up to an hour once a day are beneficial for many seniors.

This positive approach to maintaining good health works. Enjoy the benefits.

17

Delaying and Preventing Dementia

―――

Caring for a loved one suffering from a form of dementia requires having and understanding the diagnosis, the course the illness follows and prognosis of the specific dementia. The most common type is Alzheimer's Disease (AD) that comprises between 60 to 80% of all dementias and is the one that has cast fear in the minds of spouses and family members. The second most prevalent form is vascular dementia and occurs following a major stroke, but may appear as well by the individual's experiencing a series of small strokes that eventually lead to dementia, albeit slowly. The diagnosis may be unclear, since an early onset of Alzheimer's may also accompany the small strokes.

Other causes of dementia may include: Parkinson's Disease, Huntington's Disease, Frontotemporal dementia, Dementia with Lewy

Bodies and traumatic brain injury. An early form of dementia, Mild Cognitive Impairment (MCI) may be a precursor to Alzheimer's. Since many cases of dementia can be treated, primarily MCI, which when treated, could slow down the onset of AD, it is important to determine the diagnosis of an affected person. Be aware of the **early** symptoms of dementia that include: memory loss, communication and language difficulties, lack of attentiveness, reduced reasoning ability and problems in socializing. For all cases of dementia, the importance of seeing a physician for diagnosis and treatment can't be overstressed.

Since dementia may eventually affect almost half of living adults then it behooves all of us to understand how to slow down the potential of developing dementia and even preventing it during our individual life spans. Perhaps the earliest form of care giving is educating oneself, spouses and family members on the care of one's mental and physical selves. Number one on this list is caring for yourself. Loving yourself and putting the odds on your side in order to avoid mental deterioration later in life should dictate your lifestyle. By following the suggestions listed below you will have taken that step. As a bonus, you will live a far healthier life and have more self-pride in your personal accomplishments. At the same time, you can foster and even work together with your spouse and family to spread your zeal in maintaining good health.

Some may want to determine if they are genetically handicapped by DNA studies in order to learn if they have the APOE e4 gene, double or single and believe they are destined to get AD. Don't assume that must occur, since everyone having the gene does not get AD. Remember, no one knows in advance if AD will strike. Just don't live in fear of it happening.

What can we do to try to prevent or slow down Alzheimer's once it has become manifest? Various studies indicate that the onset of AD can be postponed, sometimes for years, and maybe prevented, by following certain guidelines.

All older people should carefully evaluate the following factors and follow them, if at all possible.

1. Treat diabetes, type two, vigorously and continuously.

2. Treat depression and other psychological problems, such as loneliness, self-doubt and fears of any type.

3. Maintain a physically active life. Aerobic exercise is especially effective for the mind, as well as the body.

4. Keep the mind active through mental games, such as crossword puzzles, bridge, chess, reading, and others. Mentally challenging and stimulating activities of all types are advised to diminish the risk of MCI.

5. Check medications that have been connected to mental changes, such as heart and psychiatric medicines.

6. Avoid ingesting food exposed to insecticides. Many animals ingest them as part of eating food that has been sprayed. It may be preferable to buy organic foods.

7. Check for lead in paint chips and dust near old homes painted with lead paint, which is especially potent in causing brain inflammation, a major factor in developing dementia.

8. Be careful in doing exercises in smog areas as the components of smog are especially harmful.

9. Maintain a well-documented diet that includes low saturated fat, little or no red meats, stop eating refined grains and excess sugar. Your diet should be similar to the Mediterranean Diet, with fish, especially cold water fish, such as salmon, sardines, mackerel, and tuna, that provide high levels of omega-3-fatty acids. Other parts of the diet include nuts, poultry and especially predominantly dark and green vegetables, fruits (high in colorful varieties), all berries, especially blueberries, blackberries, strawberries and raspberries. The studies involving healthy diets are increasingly conclusive that such diets delay or ward off AD.

Most important is **believing** that your efforts to delay the onset of dementia and to slow its progress will be effective. Having a positive mental attitude as you both fight the onset, and the condition itself is the most essential part of your fight for health. The following article offers additional methods for understanding and prevention of dementia.

18

Overcoming the Fear of Dementia Using Mental Imagery

Despite one's accomplishments and continuing activities, a day comes when your aging brain taps you on the shoulder and whispers, "Don't get too cocky, you're no different than others." We all arrive at a time when despite our most determined wish to always remain young that eventually we do get old. You imagine pictures of the elderly staring without seeing, searching for a word. You shudder and think, "Poor soul, Alzheimer's again." So the purpose of this article has been set. Those attitudes have to go.

Almost all people as they get older undergo normal changes in mental and physical abilities, such as memory retention, judgment and mental aliveness. When such changes occur, we may develop a fear that early dementia has come into our life.

When a person has truly entered the realm of early dementia the changes become obvious and appropriate treatment can and should be sought. Seeking reassurance from your family doctor often relieves understandable anxiety as diagnosis and treatment are assessed.

What I am about to suggest is that we undertake a special approach using both literal and symbolic mental imagery to open our brains to the formidable power of our imagination and imagery. Does mental imagery work? Absolutely. Does it work with dementia? Unknown. But it **works well with fear** and has been useful in many areas of both mental and physical activities. Many athletes have used mental imagery and find improvement when they perform the same action on the field. Mental imagery has also been used in many psychosomatic conditions, such as: controlling eating, overcoming headaches, and treating depression and anxiety. The use of Positron Emission Topography (PET) has clearly demonstrated specific changes occur in the brain. The brain records the mental and the physical action as similar or identical.

Today, I am taking a leap of faith and will introduce a series of mental exercises to be practiced daily, as a way of warding off the onset of dementia. I want to be clear from the beginning that I have no way of knowing if this will work. You must use it on faith. You **must believe in its value** without ever knowing if it will prevent or inhibit the onset of dementia. If you use it for the next ten years and discover that you are entering the early stages of dementia does that mean you wasted ten years of time. Of course not, since the very act of spending what would amount to about five minutes a day gave you an entirely new sense of self and brightened your outlook on life. From the imagery, you gained a belief that your mind was getting younger, changed how you pranced around, gave you the impetus to do more physically and, above all, **overcame your fear** that you were in the hopeless grip of the passage of time.

You are about to create a very positive belief system or mindset that you have the mental power to influence the development of your brain. It will involve mental attitudes that determine who you are and how you function as a human being.

The exercises are done while sitting quietly in a chair (never in a car) with eyes closed and breathing slowly and normally. You can use literal imagery (actual object as blood vessels) or symbolic imagery, using symbols for real objects (such as pipes for blood vessels).

Imagery exercise No. 1

Visualize seeing blood flowing through the blood vessels in the brain (interconnecting pipes) increasing and bathing the brain in super-abundant oxygen. **Feel** your brain becoming more alive; you become brighter, knowing your brain is being super nourished.

Exercise No. 2

Again, see the blood vessels. This time the blood is coursing through your brain and washing away all impurities, including amyloids, leaving your brain pristine, the brain of a very young person. You exult in feeling more alert, younger, and alive.

Exercise No. 3

Focus on your negativity especially any **fears** you carry related to beliefs you are developing dementia. Tell yourself, **absolutely convincingly**, that you do not have dementia and are preventing yourself from ever developing it. You will no longer have any fear related to such false beliefs.

Exercise 4. End-state imagery.

Imagine yourself living in the future, perpetually younger, walking with a spring in your steps, enthusiasm in your bearing. Imagine that you feel and are more youthful, have sparkling eyes, higher voice and no aging squeaks. You repeat to yourself that you will never be old again.

Finally, I suggest that all older people with an eye to healthy longevity, independent of a fear of dementia do these exercises. Do them three to five times a day. Each series will take about one minute. You will gain a lifetime of heightened vitality.

19

Are You Worried About Alzheimer's?

"What's going on, Marilyn, you look so glum?" Sheila gently asked her close friend.

"I don't want to talk about it and anyway I'm probably way out of line with my feelings."

"Ok, what's the matter?"

"Sheila, I think that Dave's getting Alzheimer's Disease."

"Really?"

"Well, he does forget things and now he is exhibiting some strange behavior."

"Like what?"

"Well, for example, you know we share making dinner every night and we each do certain things that makes it easy for us. Now, at times, he seems to forget the sequence. Once he came into the kitchen to help me start dinner and looked puzzled. He asked me if I needed anything. It was obvious he didn't know why he was there. I felt on several occasions that he didn't seem to know where he was."

"Anything else?"

"I really got worried when I walked into his office to see if he wanted some tea and maybe take a break for lunch and he hurriedly erased whatever he was watching on his computer. I jokingly asked if he was enjoying watching some pretty girls in a porno video."

"Well, maybe that question bothered him."

"No, no, not that. We often joke about sex ads and sexy performances in movies. No, he wasn't hiding anything sexual. I tell you he became so flustered I became worried about what was going on."

"So what did he finally tell you?"

"That's the trouble. He became flustered and kept saying it was nothing. At first, I tried cajoling him, saying he was keeping secrets from me."

"It wasn't even funny to him. But in an aggravated and I thought in a frightened voice, he said, 'Stop bugging me'. He didn't even remember what he was watching."

"He said that?"

"Yes."

"Maybe he was joking."

That's what I wondered; however, he put his head between his hands but not before I think I saw tears in his eyes."

"What is going on here?" Elaine backed off from hard questioning

"I don't know but there are other things going on and I'm worried that he may be coming down with Alzheimer's."

Have you discussed the problem with him?"

"No, I don't want him to think I'm worried."

"Marilyn, you're doing him a disservice. Let's assume he is showing the first signs of Alzheimer's. There may be drugs he can take that will be more useful now than if you wait."

"Elaine, when you had to put Bob into an Assisted living facility because of his dementia, I know how much you went through for several years before he finally just couldn't remember anything and was always getting lost. What can I do? I'm so worried."

"You need to talk to him."

I can't. He's a worry-wart kind of man and if he thinks I believe he has dementia it might make him worse."

"Marilyn, I suggest you watch him for a few weeks and try to observe if he shows any other signs of Alzheimer's.'

"Like what?"

"Naturally his memory. But more important whether he becomes confused about anything. Does his judgment seem faulty? Does he do anything that seems wrong or dangerous or inappropriate? If you asked him to dry dishes or boil eggs or take the thrash to the bin outside, does he follow through."

"Ok, I can watch him more closely and not laugh off anything odd."

"Also, does he easily engage in conversations with you and others and make sense. Especially does he laugh at the right times; does he show humor; is he continually attentive; or does he just grow silent or become agitated?

"Does he avoid doing independent things or does he appear to just follow you around?

""Marilyn, you need to find out what's going on. Always keep in mind. Worry itself can cause many of the symptoms of dementia and unless treated can really trouble and handicap a person. You've got to narrow this down to the point where you can finally discuss it with him and, if there is doubt, insist, for his own peace of mind, that he sees a physician. You can start with your primary care doctor or if he's willing, go directly to a referred specialist to evaluate him. Always be aware that until he is convinced, he doesn't have it, almost anything you do can intensify his symptoms. And if you have caught the early stages of Alzheimer's or other dementia then early treatment can truly benefit him."

"Thanks so much, Elaine," Marilyn said softly, tears in her eyes as she hugged her friend.

20

The Caregivers and Alzheimer's

Alzheimer's can reveal its presence at any age though most likely after 70 and certainly by the 80's. When present, the illness gradually advances and slowly robs loved ones of their identity and ability to relate. The need of constant care becomes apparent. The early symptoms warn the family and the sufferer since Alzheimer's victims are aware of the changes they are undergoing. However, as behavioral and personal changes accelerate, the caregiver becomes tied full time watching the loved one, always attentive to prevent accidents, falls and getting lost. In later stages, the loss of bodily controls and inability to eat alone intensify the needs of the caregiver.

As deterioration continues, a time comes when the caregivers and others are no longer recognized and physical deterioration mounts. No one who has not experienced such change can enter the mind of a caregiver. Her (or his) life has been upended with no end in sight. As the months and years go by, caregivers have varying reactions. Some become overwhelmed with the obligations and endless needs of their loved one and become angry even wishing the death of the suffering person who is often no longer aware of time, place or people from his real life. Such strong negative feelings are often accompanied by guilt. Others reach out by developing a greater or at least a different kind of love for the disappearing person. Some become increasingly empathic as they face their own questions of death, and the chance that the same could happen to them.

Some caregivers cry incessantly trying to hide their grief and torment and ambivalence. Often as they lie at night in the same bed and want to reach out and hold and hug the person they love, tears stream down their face, even as they whisper "I love you." Perhaps initially, their lover responded and they hugged and even kissed, but time moves incessantly and the connection unwinds, until they are hugging an empty body and only tears suffice. Many caregivers now experience a form of love and giving unknown until the intimacy they knew had disappeared. Their love had attained a spiritual meaning. Some caregivers enter an unknown world of spirit and God and even believe their life has been blessed.

At times, the stress rises to a level where the caregiver suffers enormously. He or she tends to withdraw and avoids people and loses interest in any form of activities. Depression occurs and can deepen to a point of despair and even hopelessness. Considering the intensity of constant care giving and watching the inner dying of a loved one, stress is understandable. At times, the struggle between guilt of wanting to be free and the underlying love becomes unbearable and the caregiver must be relieved of his/her obligation. The support of an assisted living facility must be sought.

How does a caregiver find that inner strength and perseverance to care for a loved one over years, especially when the "real" person has disappeared into his or her illness?

1. For relaxation and inner reflection caregivers benefit by engaging in daily meditation. During meditation the caregiver should bring up memories of love and the experiences of the past that brought love to them.

2. Acknowledge both the burden of caring and simultaneously the giving of love and nurturing to your loved one. Find the balance of giving and taking care of yourself.

3. Make clear during the meditation that a time will come when you must relinquish your total responsibility and welcome help, including letting your loved one leave you.

4. Be aware that visits to your loved one after leaving their home will be for love but not for you to also suffer. Many times, visits are too prolonged when the AD patient is no longer aware of anything in his environment. Prepare for such events long before they occur.

5. Don't feel guilty if you imagine your loved one's death. In the dire moments of extreme illness, imagining or wishing for the death of the ill person is commonplace and understandable. You must work to prevent yourself from succumbing to distress as your loved one worsens and eventually dies.

6. Always be willing to accept assistance and know when it is time to let go. You are offering a ripened love; the loved one, conscious or otherwise is grateful. However, you must take realistic steps to

prevent your own suffering as you live out this period of the loss of your loved one. Know yourself. Believe in your love. Maintain your personal strength. Know when to seek help for yourself when your stress has mounted and before you fall prey to guilt, a sense of despair or the emptiness that comes with loss.

Love yourself as you maintain the steadiness of your caring even as your stress mounted. You have also done a vital service for family unity.

21

Lightening the Caregiver's Burdens

Living with a handicapped person suffering with a form of incipient or even moderately advanced dementia, such as Alzheimer's, or Parkinsonism or other incapacitating illness places a burden upon the caregiver. Other changes due to aging, such as weakness, balance issues, cancer or an unrelenting dependency on drugs, can upset a person's equilibrium and change one's perspective about life. These conditions are commonplace as we age. Often both partners of a couple relationship have one or more of them in varying degrees of severity though one is usually worse. One partner then becomes the caregiver.

The more severely ill person tends to become dependent on the love, caring and kindness of the other. Considerable time is required to give their loved one what is needed. The caregiver is constantly evaluating what needs to be done, potential dangers, can their spouses or partners be left alone or do they need constant care. Is the condition advancing rapidly or not?

In addition, we need to constantly keep alert to our own need of medical help, perhaps even finding our own caregiver. Such complex situations affect many seniors. With aging, the loss of energy, the concern over the worsening of a pervasive health issue such as diabetes, cardiac problems, gastro-intestinal disorders, mental conditions and new symptoms suggestive of cancer are ever gnawing at our consciousness.

Do such situations prevent living without worry, and being able to direct our lives toward one of happiness and to find ways to transform our lives to a more creative existence? The answer is a qualified NO. Everyone in a situation as I have described must overcome the tendency to become negative and believe his/her life has or will become restrictive. Many of us will be involved with these important and even life-threatening conditions, now or in the future. Once you accept that your life is primarily one of being a caregiver then even taking time for self-growth and personal fulfillment may be tinged with guilt. Love and guilt tie you to your obligation. Separation and self-direction seem to be a selfish act. Your personal needs are put aside. You remain a kind, giving and loving partner or friend.

My objective is to encourage everyone that no matter what illnesses you or your loved ones have that it is possible and feasible to live a happy and creative life without neglecting self or others. As I have noted elsewhere, we live so that one day when death approaches, we can honestly say that we have lived as well as possible and do not die with memories of what we did not accomplish. Rather we state that we had encompassed and enjoyed the activities that interested us. We had developed friendships and new hobbies and actually attended more closely and lovingly to our loved ones and to ourselves. We did not neglect our loved ones, but rather we added ourselves to our list of loved ones.

How do we accomplish what I suggest?

The method is developing increasing self-awareness, a form of mindfulness that guides you to proper action in your own mind. It is essential that you are not operating under self-deception, such as hiding anger and guilt or acting to get approval or love.

Your focus will be two-fold. First, concentrate upon the symptoms and behavior of the handicapped person. Put yourself into his or her mind. Feel as deeply as you can the pain of her arthritic fingers or forgetfulness or tendency to fall or her mumbling about dying. Whatever the symptoms, through your use of mindfulness, you will now know and feel more. You have crept into the mind of the person. And you would have changed. You will discover that you have become more adept at soothing and offering help and showing love. You will have become closer and more loving.

The second part is now focusing on your inner beliefs about your feelings toward yourself. It is now time for self-nurturing. You will temporarily devote your entire energy to yourself. I suggest you go into a mindful meditation state and unhesitatingly search for any doubts or feelings that you are hurting or rejecting your loved one when you now take time to enter a personal state of creativity leading you toward transformation. Don't rush this meditation state for you may discover feelings that perhaps you hide or cover up.

Your objective is to know your truth. Keep in mind that in a mindful meditation state, you can also overcome any feelings or thoughts you find untenable. Remember that guilt and feeling that you are withdrawing love from your loved one are frequently the culprits that tie you inappropriately to your caregiving. Such negativity must be overcome. Meditation will help you.

Success at self-transformation depends on establishing a healthy equilibrium of giving love to loved ones and to yourself.

22

Overcoming the Fear of Dying

Can you talk about the end of life with humor and laughter, coupled with the feeling that you have lived a good life? How about your reaction to my using the word dying or death? Only words! But words that often convey emotion, fear, and strange thoughts, such as, "where do I go from here?"

We all need to look at the final chapter of life, i.e. death, as inevitable that needs to be accepted with equanimity. However, for many people the approach of death instead brings fear, which tends to increase as aging proceeds and may reach the point of obsession for people in their 70s, 80s and 90s. Especially affected are those who have lived unfulfilled, feeling they wasted many of their previous years and never having accomplished what they intended or desired. Some spend their adult lives working in unsatisfying jobs or professions or live in an impoverished marriage or no marriage at all. Love eludes many and many are still seeking true spirituality in their search for a connection to God. Unfulfilled older people, who feel their final days slipping away, may live for years unable to overcome their fear of dying.

Now is the time to reexamine your life and find ways to overcome your fears and cultivate a life free of such fears. The path to live peacefully with our inevitable death depends on believing that each day you live will be meaningful by your becoming active and creative, while seeking new venues and new pursuits. You can consciously determine that you will replace a fear of dying with thoughts of finding more fulfilling ways to live, no matter what your age. And when death comes knocking at the door you can welcome it into your home and say that you are ready to leave the earth; you have lived your life, knowing you will never really die in the hearts of those who loved you and you loved.

Although paths of fulfillment are many and choices are bountiful, I would like to suggest that you include seeking out the beauty of nature, walking among trees, or on the beach, listening to much loved music, and exploring music unheard. Have you listened to the Mozart piano sonatas recently or Joan Baez or Enya? Picking up and rereading loved books, or rediscovering poetry will bring a new feeling of belonging and love into your life.

The question of health often interferes with ending our life peacefully. Dying in the throes of illness, such as cancer, heart disease, Alzheimer's, and other painful conditions changes the scenario. In conditions where pain has disrupted a peaceful ending of life then the treatment of the pain is essential. If the ending of life takes place in a hospital or outside hospice versus one's home, the conditions have also changed.

What I propose now is in all situations when death is near that we have faith in our own mental ability to guide us through this period. The coming of death should be peaceful. Frequently, the following imagery exercises done in just a few minutes several times a day can foster the sought-after peace and joy that you deserve in your final days.

Close your eyes while sitting in a chair or lying in bed. Breathe normally.

1. If you believe in an **afterlife** that includes Heaven, imagine that you enter Heaven and are greeted by angels and perhaps those you have loved that have preceded you. Immerse yourself in this vision, **believe it**, and feel your doubts and fears leave and that dying will bring you peace and happiness.

2. If you believe in the **immortality of your soul** and reincarnation use the following imagery. Visualize your soul leaving your body when you die and entering a new realm filled with beautiful flowers, trees, birds and animals. Other souls freely float by and greet you with love. You know that you will remain in this other realm until God calls you to another body.

3. If you are preparing to die **without any belief in an afterlife**, visualize yourself without any fear, anxiety, doubts or guilt as you imagine the many accomplishments that fulfilled your life. Love and joy in the life you have led remain strongly etched in your thoughts as you imagine your death.

How you die depends on your attitude. Believe in the inevitability of your becoming nonexistent and when that time approaches you will leave life without regrets, knowing you tried to have lived as well as possible, accomplished as much as you were able and left behind memories of you in both real terms and in forms of love and friendships. Remember that you play a part in the manner that you die. Make your final days peaceful and joyful.

23

The Joy of Treasure Seeking

There it is. I found it. What a prize! What luck! The exclamations of lucky explorers, the searchers who find treasures everywhere in their multiple wanderings. These are individuals whose eyes are always wide open, darting here and there. They roam down the narrowest alleyways always poking through vendor's bins and carts. Much of the fun is in the looking and finding many items that they admire, but do not purchase. Then you find that unique object in the most unlikely place or when you have almost abandoned looking for that day or on that trip. **Heaven in a teacup**, an old cliché, but that's what it is.

Where are all the likely places for discovery? The simplest answer is anywhere in the world. Any country, city, hidden flea market, gatherings of people eager to sell their no longer desired treasures that may become yours. Looking near your home makes these discoveries frequent and makes every trip you take special. Just recently, my wife and I found a marvelous, exquisitely carved wooden vase waiting for us in a lonely corner of a Target store, hidden among large wooden baskets and trays. My wife noticed it out of the corner of her eye and picked it up and called me over. At that moment, we knew we had discovered a beautiful vase that would fit perfectly in our home.

Most of us do find souvenirs of our travels and often bring back clothes, scarves and jewelry specifically sought out based on the area of travel. No doubt, these items add to our life but it is not what I am addressing. No, it is the **unusual object**, the special one of a kind art piece, not the painting you found as you were cruising galleries. They are also special, but different from that piece that caught your eye and was not at all what you were seeking. The beauty and genius of the maker were what stood out. Perhaps hundreds of other travelers passed it by. No matter. For you it was like a star burst. And if it is shared by your lover, if you travel as a couple, then look it over, touch it, and if you can't live without it and it is within your price budget, buy it.

On one occasion traveling in Vermont my wife and I stumbled on a small shop where a single ball of glass enclosing incredible and imaginative forms, part of a small window display, stopped us. The pull was there so into the store we went and discovered that this was the one store in the nation that carried what we called **spirit balls** created by a Canadian artist. We became friendly with the owner of the shop, a delightful woman, who surrounded herself with many kinds of glass pieces. Irene and I decided to buy one of the small number of spirit balls.

What happened then was kind of a miracle. We asked the proprietress if we could take one of the balls outside to see the effect of sunlight shining through the glass. Her response was" which one?"

Having no immediate favorite, she suggested taking out all eight and in short order she transferred the bases that carried the balls and lined them up outside protected by strategically placed chairs. **Just imagine this scene.** The entire sidewalk outside her store displayed these marvelous art pieces. For almost one-half hour, Irene and I stared and reflected as we sought the one that spoke loudest to us. We heard its voice, as we finally selected the glass ball that now rests in our home.

With a sense of vivacity, I besiege you to go out with your eyes open and your heart responsive and nothing specific in your mind but with **total openness**. When that special moment arrives and you stare unbelievably at a tiny carved Buddha or a multi-colored candy bowl or a picture hanging for sale on the wall of a restaurant just above your head don't turn away. Absorb it. The delight is in your reaction whether you walk away with it or without it. You might be in San Francisco, or New York or in Cost Plus or Pier One, or in South Africa or Paris. Makes no difference, it is the **open eyes and ready heart** to see and to love that brings a treasure into your life. Over the years, your collection will grow and you will be surrounded with your personal wonderland that has become alive in your serendipitous discoveries.

This article is about **discovery**, searching, getting to know an art piece and loving it. Your lives will change and your surroundings will sing songs to you forever. Ah yes, that vase from Target, I think it might look better over here, Irene sang out.

24
Discoveries as a Way of Life

As we age, we need to find ways to stimulate our mind and enhance our sense of life. Becoming more lively, adding sparkle to our very existence and above all making our life more stimulating and upbeat is essential to bringing more fun than we could have possibly imagined into our senior world.

Since most of us start the day with a healthy and appealing breakfast, we have a natural opportunity to make our first discovery of the day. In addition to eating, breakfast entails other activities. We might begin with the news on TV or by reading the daily newspaper and discussing the news with your partner if you live with someone. As is my custom, I put a CD on our stereo that we haven't heard for years. Perhaps it will be Dixieland or New Orleans jazz or one of the jazz giants, such as Albert Ammons, whose boogie woogie is without parallel. I sometimes fall back on music of Mozart that I may have never heard, such as his church sonatas, or one of his early symphonies. On other occasions, we listen to the wonderful nocturnes of the Irish composer John Fields or one of the 104 delightful symphonies of Haydn that have waited to be heard. All discoveries. All awakenings. Without fail, the music calls forth memories or feelings of the past. The nostalgia that touches us sometimes brings tears to our eyes. Such moments are priceless. My wife and I, as talkative as we are, are often silent as we become absorbed in the music. In today's world, Pandora offers untold music choices in place of personal CD's.

Breakfast is over. What else can you do? Opening your eyes and mind to a variety of discoveries, the pepper-uppers, I might call them. The list can be long or short, depending how adventurous you are. Since most of you take walks at times, my first suggestion is to devote your curiosity and explorer attitude to the many things that exist on average streets that will be noteworthy on a 30-minute walk.

The first object that might catch your eye would be an unusual tree, one with an exotic shape or animal-like branches. One morning, as I was admiring the prancing deer that sprang from the trunk of a formidable oak tree, I heard a wonderful song tweeted by a blue winged bird on another tree, and I turned to view it, even as it flew off. So beautiful, I thought as I continued walking. In front of me in the middle of the street, a proud turkey flashed its wide circular tail hoping to attract a female who was scurrying out of his reach not many feet ahead. I couldn't help but smile, easily reacting to the romantic scene ahead. I waited until they moved to the adjoining meadow and sauntered out of sight.

Within a few minutes, I greeted another walker and her frisky Maltese who came over for a pat. At that moment, two small deer frolicking on the hillside ran down to the street to say hello before they crossed. I walked on and approached three crows standing on the sidewalk eyeing me warily as I gave them wide berth. I moved on. They flew off.

Overhead, fluffy, curvy, brilliantly white clouds floated languorously. As is my usual tendency, I searched for unique faces staring down at me and found a few. They are always there. I took several deep breaths and reflected on the wonders and the miracle of just being alive. I strolled on and thought of the day ahead.

I thought of arranging to take my wife to dinner that evening to visit one of our favorite restaurants and enjoy the warm welcome offered from the servers and owners who have come to know us as patrons and now as friends. Irene and I gradually come to know individual servers by inquiring about their lives or feelings. We genuinely respond to their menu suggestions and ask for advice. In certain small restaurants, we order the same dishes and the server often remembers our orders. We return because we love the food and enjoy the ambience and the special welcome, much as we like visiting favorite friends in their home. We feel that we have extended our home to encompass these outside dining experiences.

What is this article all about? It's how we see and react to the world and to recognize that much of our joy comes from the interaction. It's how we bring passion to our activities and discussions when alone or with others. Seeing change and being able to view the good and bad, the beautiful and the ugly, opening your mind to everything and to always act kindly toward yourself. New discoveries are like balm for the mind. Soothing, yet stimulating, awakening and expanding, opening endless worlds to enter.

25

The Search for Love

Love beckons us, calls to us in almost unlimited ways at all ages and in never-ending styles and forms. Love poems describe the lures, the heartbreaks, the dreams, the unrequited love and the perfect love that almost happened. When we have not let frustration deter us, dreams of our elusive soul mate is at the top of the list and hopes. By the time, we have reached our senior years, we have generally enjoyed a number of love relationships, including, perhaps, finding a soul mate. Some seniors continue to live with one. Others live in love relationships rarely experiencing long periods of being alone. Many more have deep and loving friends to share their lives. Some, however, live alone, frequently after the death of a spouse or a divorce when they could not find or did not want to find a new lover and companion.

I want to address the large number of singles who desire to find love. Most know the various paths they could take and have probably gone those routes. Nevertheless, there is some value in describing the many ways that singles can bring love into their lives. Let's start with the way that relationships of seniors unfold. Meeting can be by chance in a line at the market, or by pursuing dates in a dating service, such as Match.com, or by introduction through a friend, or meeting at a club or a dance or while traveling.

By actively pursuing dating most will find new companions, friends, sexual partners and even bona fide, lifelong lovers. However, most searches, as when you were younger and single, result in more casual and superficial relationships. For many, the idea of finding pure, enveloping and transforming love, may appear a bit challenging. Perhaps in the past, you had found a deeply spiritual soul mate only to discover that the relationship was evanescent and in a moment of crisis, experienced its dissolution. The search for true and open love and the sharing of one's innermost beliefs may seem too unlikely and therefore not worth pursuing. However, for dreamers and with the willingness to remain alert to the possibility of it happening, surprises may come at any time and age.

If, indeed, you continue to seek a meaningful, even a deep love relationship, such as a soul mate, how would you know when you have met that person? That can be a difficult question to answer, but often begins with special feelings developing between two people. Finding a soul mate usually does not start by falling in love at first sight. That is infatuation with sexual feelings dominating. More likely, it starts as a friendship that may lead to a love relationship. A soul mate evolves out of a unique connection that two people make usually after knowing each other for a time, although the time involved is quite variable. The essential ingredients involve an openness and willingness to reveal one's deepest and often hidden secrets and desires. Soul mates also share core beliefs, which may involve music, art, literature, love of books, theater, similar feelings toward children, religion, politics and possibly a love of sports. In other words, a true soul mate is one who shares many of the important elements in lifestyle, communication, beliefs and meaningful activities. Another important dimension is the deep respect and real support for each other's separate interests.

Couples have varying abilities to face deep-seated conflicts. Unless they have similar insight and both desire to probe deeply within themselves, they usually relate by discussing issues that are on the surface. This level of communication offers a reasonable degree of intimacy compared to couples who avoid issues that include even surface feelings. Men who have been taught to keep feelings submerged even when their love is clearly enunciated tend to react by doing and showing rather than telling. This can be observed with male friends who relate to each other through action versus women friends who are much more likely to relate through feelings. By discussing these differences couples can become more intimate. For example, a woman who attends a sport event her husband loves can engage him in explaining his feelings about why the game is so meaningful to him. Surprisingly, many men enjoy an in depth discussion about their love of sports.

So, in your search for love, seek a partner who will provide the friendship, companionship and love accompanied by mutual respect. Don't miss out on finding that wonderful companion who will embellish and augment your senior years by waiting indefinitely for that elusive soul mate. As your search continues, most important is realizing that in the process, you will bring new friends into your life who will also help you attain the sought after peace, love, fulfillment and spiritual contentment you deeply desire and deserve.

26

A Rolling Leaf

A rolling leaf caught the tail end of a wind curling up the street and blew uphill while most of the world around it was still. That is how we move forward. We pick up the slightest stimulation and encouragement, add a little push from our ready mind and feel our heart pulsate. The creative soul has awakened. The adventurous and happy traveler is on the move.

The outside breeze has quieted to a mere unheard whisper and the wind has snuggled up to our imagination. Then in a sudden stroke it blows with increasing velocity as it takes our mind and guides it to wondrous places. We are the wind. We blow at will. We are the masters of our lives; we are the masters of what we bring forth; we are the masters who create our happiness and fulfillment; we are the masters of who we are and who we will be.

What is this wind that blows within and stirs us to action and fulfillment? Can I light a match and see the glow of embers penetrate my inner being and come alive? Is that an awakening? Can I make a wish and see the birth of a new creation? How do I stir my creative soul? Around where I stand, spring out flowers and trees; I smile, for creativity is already alive. I am part of the awakening. I turn inward and search. I want to see, know in the fullest sense, my creative self. I want aliveness.

For a brief time, I stand utterly still. I breathe deeply. I free my mind of control. I will my thoughts to come freely. I want to expose my inner self. I close my eyes though the darkness of evening has already clouded my vision. My thoughts have become beacons of light. From these moments I spout a poetic utterance. So simple, as I merely put the feelings of my heart into words.

The moon stares down from high above and whispers words of love.
My heart enraptured reaches out to the moon's unerring light,
I look down the long moon-brightened path no ending in sight.
My mind's come alive bathed by the celestial light.
I love you, dear moon, I love you.

How can I give to you, the reader, an understanding of the simplicity that brought those words to consciousness? No more or less than your mind is alive, bubbling with anticipation, a feeling you are vitally alive. You must believe that such risings exist in all of us. We each control our switches

When you next stroll the quiet streets, notice all the rolling leaves and birds, "mind" the gifts of Heaven for they will stir your inner world to bring forth the feelings, the words sought by your heart as it again awaits to burst forth with the song of poetry. Today I am writing these words so that all of us can write poetry. Poetry comes so easily. I have talked and written about it before and I will again. Walking, sitting, lying in bed, eyes open, eyes closed, pencil in hand, or only in your mind. The thoughts can be beautiful or evanescent or made up without form. There is no wrong in writing poetry. Anyone, adult or child can do it. Think of any moment and write it down. Now is that moment. The dusk has come and the shadows are falling. Even as light fades, my world brightens. My chest is filled with deep, filling and wholesome breaths. The words flow into my mind.

A tiny blue and yellow bird flies the sky singing songs of love.
It darts here and there and catches my eye,
To my shoulder it comes, and lands and stays,
Tenderly, that tiny bird kisses my lips, my eyes fill with tears.
The moonlit night has brought you to me, dearest bird.
The moonlit night has brought love to me.

You can start a hundred poems. A single line or hundreds will speak your thoughts and open your heart. You can tell an entire story in a few quatrains or write a novel in iambic pentameter. You bring into the world your illumination: what is and what will be. You make choices. You create or not. You forgive or not. You love or not. You reach out or not. You live as a vital, kind, giving and caring soul or not. You create your poems of life or not. You make the choice or not.

Dear friends, above all else, cast aside negative choices. Make all decisions favor truth and personal growth. See and follow the vision of enlightenment and fulfillment. Living in happiness and contentment is your reward.

27

All the World's a Stage

"All the world's a stage, and all the men and women merely players. They have their exits and their entrances; And one man in his time plays many parts." (*As You Like It Act 2, Scene 7*)

Ah, Shakespeare, your words are golden and send shimmers into our hearts. We mere mortals living out our time and playing our roles on stage after stage have entered upon an age when jeopardy has entered our world. We, however, are the intrepid ones and fear not our final part, our final role. One day, our lives' adventures will have come to an end and we will leave the earth in joy.

We will live our lives finding new areas to explore and venture forth into exciting, even captivating, worlds. We will boldly determine the level of fulfillment and creativity we bring into our lives. We don't fear or back away, but stand strong. As Shakespeare eloquently stated, "Cowards die many times before their deaths; the valiant never taste of death but once." (*Julius Caesar Act 2, Scene 2*). And for us the taste will be good for we will have lived to our fullest.

Initiating new and varied paths to discoveries and eventual achievement, the personal emphasis is knowing yourself. Penetrate all barriers and know your strengths and weaknesses. Shakespeare in a few words "To thine own self be true." (*Hamlet Act 2, Scene 2*) points out the essence of self-knowledge, so essential to finding those elusive activities that will bring light to your life. Hamlet, so filled with wisdom as he struggled with his own doubts and wishes for revenge, knew that over thinking could set in motion a false action or an error in judgment. He reflected deeply as he uttered the simple words, "There is nothing either good or bad, but thinking makes it so." (*Hamlet Act 1, Scene 3*). Does over thinking on a troubling subject give rise to resolution or to proper action? We know that obsessing or merely pondering too long on any important subject can lead to false beliefs if personal defenses, such as denial or displacement of the real intent of the conflict, occur.

Facing conflict with the tenacity of a bulldog is essential to gaining personal truth, but changes are occurring in our world where the rumbles of doubt and troubles of antagonism may arise. Shakespeare knew that at any time truth can be questioned and may become a weapon that can strike you. Around you may appear individuals who turn against you, but much more likely is that some part of yourself may rear up to trip you, even cause you to close your eyes to truth and adopt untruth. We have found such untruths and misinformation and deception increasingly prevalent in our society much as Shakespeare revealed in his plays.

In certain plays, the use of deception creates the action and taxes our credulity. How can we believe that Othello so in love with Desdemona believes the treacherous Iago? His lack of suspicion of Iago's motives, the misinformation, stretches our belief even as we are caught up in the deception.

What do we make of Viola in love with Duke Orsino in *Twelfth Night* who courts Countess Olivia for the Duke. Olivia falls in love with Viola disguised as a boy but, when expedient, quickly shifts her affections to Sebastian. Her switch and belief served her well as she now had a bona fide lover. I certainly must mention the wily Falstaff who lies at every turn in his attempt to control and deceive Hal. Shakespeare knew human nature and how we are fed by misinformation, how easily our consciences are compromised, that there can be many truths describing every event. He did not hesitate to use external influences to change attitudes and love. Remember the mischievous Puck who drops a love potion into the eyes of people sleeping in the forest. When awakened they switch their affections to a different lover forsaking their true love.

In this period, when the political environment of our country and actually much of the world is revealing radical changes, extreme political differences have cast a shadow of confusion over our country. What are our best interests? Our relationship with the rest of the world is also changing. Our future has become clouded by bias and deception much as King Lear was duped by lying and unloving daughters and was unable to recognize truth from untruth.

Today we seek ways to determine truth. As Julius Caesar stated, "Men at some time are masters of their fates. The fault, dear Brutus, is not in our stars. But in ourselves, that we are underlings." (*Act 1, Scene 2*). That time is now. Deception and misinformation must end. Truth must prevail.

Unless our nation opens its eyes to see through the clouds that are darkening our world, we may follow the paths of Lear or Macbeth. Each of us has a choice. The future landscape of America hangs in the balance.

28
Who Am I?

Who am I? A strange question? Do I really know who I am? Am I the face that stares back at me from a mirror? What if I was that young disfigured child, Auggy, from the movie "Wonder" who was born with an ugly and misshapen face that required 20 surgeries to give him a face with eyes, nose and mouth pieced together on borrowed skin. Until he reached age ten, he hid his ugliness by wearing a robot's space helmet. At the pleading and urging of his parents to face the real world and finally go to school, he took it off. Would I have had the guts to finally remove it?

I walked with him on that first day when he held back his tears and courageously walked into the school trying not to react to the gawking, stunned children who moved out of his path and stared with horror on their faces. As I watched this extraordinary film and his slow, painfully slow, acceptance by other children and finally by himself, I knew that I was seeing much of the world's children struggling to become whole. Every child needed to learn that being different, even strangely odd, did not make him less a human, or a person who did not need love and understanding. By viewing the film, it was a very tiny leap to put into Auggy's place all the people who feel unloved, rejected, scorned, even hated. Every person of color, those of the LGBTQ persuasion, every ethically different, racially and genetically diverse group who are cast into a degraded status.

What happens to those people? Can you put yourself into the role of anyone whose identity is questioned? Have you ever wondered, "Am I a man or a woman?"

When a person's identity is questioned, indicating a confusion of individuality, what does it do to the person indicted. Is he a she or she a he? A person could be highly creative and believe he is empty. A powerful athlete, indomitable on the field, might be easily startled by a tiny noise or a perceived threat in real life. Many actors act with absorbing presence and project an entire identity with ardor and bravado, yet off stage may be reclusive, quiet and shy. Have you ever looked into the mirror and refused to accept that the image who stares back at you is you? Can you believe that your identity is so fragile and malleable? When a person lives with a façade and truly hides from his inner self, he experiences an intense conflict that has distorted his personal vision.

Who are we in our dreams? We all dream of new realities. For brief times every night we inhabit another world with different identities, different worlds. We fly and love and kill and are fearful of being killed. Who are these other selves? Am I the person wielding the ax or the person for whom the ax is intended to strike? Am I the seducer or the one being seduced? Am I all the people in my dreams? Who is that person who sometimes screams, gets wild, angry, loses control? Am I the successful entrepreneur or the cowering colleague?

And what is my soul? Who is my soul? Where is it? Is my soul more than a composite of my inherent memories that I am born with plus my lifetime of experiences? Does it exist separate from my physical body, the belief of most people, and eventually reside with God or be reincarnated? Countless religions promise a life after death.

Despite believing in a soul, even feeling you are spiritual and/or religious does not preclude doubts and conflicts about your identity. You may still succumb to depression when you feel worthless and unlovable.

So many questions. So few answers. But one thing is clear. We all need to strengthen our identities. We need to gather the many identities that break us apart and put a boundary around them. By accepting that we are different in dreams, when depressed or feel inferior, when we pray, when we scream, when we hide from fear, when we are discriminated against, only then will we unite our multiple selves and become stronger in our beliefs. Stronger in our sense of self. We will be less likely to be demeaned, criticized and attacked. We will be less likely to be swayed by social and political demands. By focusing on overcoming emotional conflicts and strengthening our egos, we can rise above identity confusion and remain oriented to a steady and whole sense of being. Self-awareness, focusing on our consciousness and behavior, will give us insight into the various components of our personality leading to identity integration. We are all composites of various memories, experiences, varying methods of upbringing, but in the final analysis we remain capable of unity and having one soul. We are a single being.

29

The Imagination

"Imagination is more important than knowledge. For knowledge is limited to all we now know and understand, while imagination embraces the entire world, and all there ever will be to know and understand."

— Albert Einstein in his inimitable words made clear our minds must be open to explore ourselves and life.

One evening, as a nine year-old-youngster and his Mom were gazing at the splendor of the awakening full moon, they noted what appeared to be a shadow across its terrain. "Mom," the youngster called out, "the moon just frowned. It must be angry with us."

"Ricky, the moon doesn't have feelings and can't make faces at us."

"Mom, I know the moon is upset and I'm going to tell it that I like it and to not feel so badly."

"Ricky. There you go again letting your imagination plays games with you."

The moon looked down and as Ricky waved, it winked back and a smile crossed its face. Ricky said nothing but inwardly knew he and the moon had just become friends.

Above all else your imagination is the fount of your creativity. At any time, at any age you can have fun with your mind. Let's try it. Let's start by creating a story. Sit down at your computer or before a pad of paper and give it a whirl. By merely picking freely at almost any idea that pops into your mind you can begin. "Do you like my bushy tail?" the smiling squirrel asked as it approached me. Before I could respond it had crawled up my leg into my arms and sat on my shoulder as it reached down to type out his own story.

From this simple beginning can come any number of stories. I could reply "yes" or "no" or "what are you doing up here" or what's your name?" or "would you like to come for dinner and meet my dog?" BTW I'm typing as I write. No active thinking required.

How about a sudden shadow fell from the sky and covered me. In awe I looked up at a great spaceship that had suddenly appeared and a ladder was descending over me. No one else was around. As I wrote the above, I realized this came from a motion picture. No problem as this is merely the stimulus for my imagination to take off.

These simple beginnings came into my mind without any preliminary ideas or trying to write a story. I merely sat at my computer waiting for my mind to produce words, any words and as quickly as

I could, I typed them down. Entire short stories or poems or songs can rise easily from your imagination. Obviously if the ideas were stirred by another's effort, they would merely be stepping stones to begin something strictly from your own imagination. The idea is to start. You can always edit and delete. Once you become a believer in your fertile imagination you will be filled with ideas.

How does one initiate such creative use of the imagination? Let's go back into childhood when every child was capable of creating stories, alone or with a playmate. Imaginary animals, playmates, kingdoms, new parents, new worlds were readily available to their mere wish. They never wondered how they would establish these wonderful games. They just made them up. And you will do the same. When you sit before your computer or a writing pad and have a specific idea in mind just start writing. If no ideas for your story come to mind then write whatever words appear. Soon the words for your story will come. If not, continue anyway. Don't feel it is not in you or you begin to doubt yourself and develop a negativity that can lead to writer's block.

The imagination can lead to new breakthroughs in technology, cooking, art in all forms. Everyone can paint or sculpt or make jewelry. Don't compare yourself to anyone. You are doing this for your own pleasure. Many people have been surprised at the level of skill they develop in a short time. To increase your knowledge or advance your skill, take classes, read books, find teachers, find others learning to use their imagination and work together.

Most important is recognizing that the use of the imagination leads to growing younger, becoming more vibrant and enthusiastic. When you write a poem or a short story or how about a novel when you are 70, 80 or 90 or paint a picture when you had not painted before, you have created a new mental world. It all starts with using your imagination. Follow Einstein as he attached himself to a light beam and discovered a new world. Say hello to the moon as you pass it by.

30
What is Truth? The Testing of Your Beliefs

Today we examine two areas of your living environment where your truth and beliefs are being strongly tested. Both are caused by people. Both affect your health and well-being.

"Don't buy that," Anne's voice rang out as her friend, Josie, was about to put a fruit drink into her cart.

"Why not, I love, mixed orange and pineapple juice."

"But that's not juice. It's a fake. It's a drink with hardly any juice and lots of sugar. Check the label." That warning is true of many foods that seemingly are whole and nutritious and yet contain few of the ingredients that seem to be listed. Look carefully and make certain that you are getting what you believe you are buying. This is very true of grains which often claim to be made of whole grains. Example, a food that says it is made with whole grains is not the same as a food that is 100% whole grains. A food can contain whole grains but very little. The deception lies in the fact that within a loaf of bread there may be 3% whole wheat, which fulfills the listing that it contains whole grains. However, the bread is mostly white (enriched) flour. Many products indicate they are 4-grain, 9-grain, even 12 or 15 grain but are mostly white flour. Grains also contain added sugar, high fructose corn syrup and artificial ingredients. Select cereals carefully and look for those with maximal whole grains and least added sugar.

A more recent deception comes in the guise of gluten-free grains that tend to be overpriced. Most people know today to avoid over-price grains that say they are gluten-free unless they have Celiac disease or an unusual genuine sensitivity to gluten. Otherwise. there is no reason to avoid gluten-free grains.

Try to avoid buying foods that contain much, if any, saturated fat and/or trans-fat. Instead consume foods that contain primarily monounsaturated and polyunsaturated fats, the heathy fats, such as all nuts and especially peanut butter.

Beware of buying food that says "cholesterol-free" since it is no longer considered that dietary cholesterol is a major concern for health. Some people still avoid eating nutritious eggs as part of their diet. If you haven't already done so, it is time to begin enjoying your scrambled or poached eggs.

I must put in a plug to avoid buying processed foods without looking carefully at the ingredients. Always check the Nutrition Label, and note the sodium, fiber, sugar, saturated and trans-fat levels. Avoid saturated and trans-fat foods. Processed food also frequently contains various preservatives and other ingredients not necessary for your health. Many meats, such as: sausages, hot dogs, corn beef and bacon, are highly processed through curing, fermentation, smoking, adding preservatives, anything to enhance taste and appeal. Try to eat unprocessed foods, such as fresh vegetables and fruits, whole grains, lean fish and beef, and vegetable oils, as olive oil and canola oil.

Jumping from food to global warming is like taking a leap off our planet. Examining our second belief may be far more important for the continuing existence of the human race. For many years, scientists have tracked changes in atmospheric CO_2, which has moved steadily higher, from 270 to 410 during the past 150 years, following the use of fossil fuel burning. Most of this rise has been during the past 50 years. Sea level has risen as has the water temperature and the global temperature. We have experienced increasingly powerful hurricanes and more widespread droughts leading to wild fires that have devastated vast lands and thousands of structures, including the entire town of Paradise. Permafrost that covers Greenland is melting adding CO_2 and methane to the atmosphere and water to the rising sea. The vast ice cover of the Arctic has shrunk to a fraction of its previous size and the summer ice cover is now disappearing leading to the terrifying realization that if it totally disappears, we are left with water that will absorb more and more heat and rapidly increase global warming. Finally, methane, a greenhouse gas that is 80 to 100 times as potent as CO_2 is increasing, not only from production of oil and gas and manure but from the hundreds if not thousands of methane lakes throughout Siberia and the intercontinental coast. The White House refuses to recognize that global warming exists and, as a result, is removing our protective laws.

What can we do? Don't buy unhealthy food. For the climate: vote for change. Read what scientists have discovered. Increase your knowledge. Join organizations in the areas that you seek to change. Learn to know what is truth and not be swayed by bias and personal theories. Support leaders who have the understanding and courage to act against adversity and a willingness to seek and act on truth.

31
How Do We Truly Live the Good Life?

*In the end, it's not the years in your life that count.
It's the life in your years.*

— Abraham Lincoln

Living the good life has been expressed by countless writers over millennia of time. The ideas and philosophy can be simply stated. Live as though you will live forever, yet live each day as though it is your last one. Emphasize creativity, freedom, self-direction and love.

Always believe that you can overcome all obstacles, yet retain a sense of reality so that you don't hit your head against a wall in frustration when you misjudge what you can accomplish. Be willing to shift directions, establish new goals, overcome frustration, know you can overcome barriers and that the light is always ahead no matter how dark it may appear at times.

The area of creativity is a key to vital and imaginative living. Find ways to overcome blocks in creativity, procrastination and self-doubt. A key component to achieving success is to eliminate comparison with others. One's uniqueness is the sine qua non for a creative lifestyle and belief in one's self is the essential personal ingredient.

The health of your body and brain are essential to reach and maintain your optimal lifestyle. A good diet and physical exercise are required. No need to have a fancy diet. Study healthy diets. Learn what determines appropriate amounts of protein, fats and carbohydrates. I generally follow the limits suggested by the USDA, the United States Department of Agriculture. Generally eating carbohydrates, 55% of your calories, fats, 30% of your calories and preferably 25%. Also avoid saturated and trans-fat. Eat primarily monounsaturated and polyunsaturated fats, the healthy fats. Don't be fooled by the multitude of over-hyped diets. Simplicity rules. Just maintain your weight and reduce it, if feasible, if you are overweight.

Friendships, love, intimacy and sharing life are other important areas to cultivate as you strive to live the good life. Both new and old friendships are important as you continue to expand your personal life. Living alone tends to lead to loneliness and may diminish the potential of finding serenity and peacefulness as you get older.

I firmly believe that each of us can overcome all barriers to a fulfilling life. Childhood, through adolescence, adulthood and the wide-open retirement period, should only be seen as periods of transitions to a continuing and improving productive and happy life. Each phase can be the time of a person's maximum productiveness and creativity. Each phase can be the time to ever-increasing fulfillment as we move wholeheartedly into the future.

We all go through life cycles of varying lengths with death as the inevitable end of the cycle that was set in motion by our birth. Neither is controlled by us. In-between birth and death is a wonderland of opportunity. For many it is not until we enter the second half of life does the real possibility of living freely actually take place. It is a time to do everything possible to live healthfully, vitally and productively and thus make these final years, no matter how long or short, as happy and bountiful as possible. Always believe that as you age your opportunities for greater fulfillment grow. Finally, in retirement you have a new freedom that offers you a unique period to transform your life.

But always know that it is not in the final years or the earliest years or the years in-between. The time is always **now**. Each time period allows you to entertain new venues to explore, new paths to follow, new dreams to fulfill. It is your time to fulfill your life. By living in the **now** you experience your greatest energy which can be directed wherever you choose. It is the time to practice your understanding of mindfulness and tap into personal change. You will no longer only dream of a new way to be active or exercise or seek friends or plan a vacation. You will be doing what you think. Your actions and thoughts will correspond. Your efficiency will astonish you.

Believe in your ability to give back, teach others, share ideas as you claim your share of the world's history. Don't wait to extend yourself or your knowledge. As you give to others, more comes back to you. Your sense of fulfillment comes from your giving but also from the reciprocal interaction with those with whom you have extended yourself. Each relationship becomes a unique world unto itself.

Finally, the good life revolves around love. Above all else, love brightens your world. Love colors your inner life and fills the lives of those you love. Love changes your surroundings, tints all with a celestial glow. Yes, live the good life filled with love. Always.

32

Authenticity and Character

―――

Our character is what we do when no one is looking.

―H. Jackson Brown, Jr.

"Dear, be warm and kind when you greet people at the meeting."

"Don't worry, I know how to act properly. I'm the perfect guest."

"Don't hug the women too long. They don't like it."

"Get off it. I'm the perfect gentleman," he yelled, as he slammed the door and left.

His wife patiently sighed and then went through the house and picked up his clothes where he had dropped them, and the newspaper scattered on the living room floor. She then noticed his tennis shoe under the coffee table that she had almost overlooked.

What does it mean to become authentic? Isn't our daily behavior real? Alas, most of us tend to live multiple lives. We have personas, outside selves and inside selves when alone. We have working selves and playful selves. We are athletes and scared of physical contact. We can give public speeches and are afraid of revealing our intimate self to anyone, even a spouse or lover. Am I addressing most of us?

Being authentic is simply a single integrated person who is the same person in all circumstances who freely and capably adapts to his current activity. For those who hide their inner world from others and even from themselves the job ahead to become a single soul is not easy. Much easier is the task for the individual who consciously admits his need to hide his real self at times and under various circumstances.

Becoming authentic requires that a person acknowledges when he hides any part of his self. Denial is the primary weapon of deception and maintaining an inauthentic self.

Steps to take are variable and dependent on the kind of deception. Are you hiding anger and aggression by appearing benign and passive, though inwardly you are concerned by the potential to explode, often a major factor in avoiding crowds and even getting close to people as friends? Are you afraid of being unattractive and need to use aggression to experience sex? Do you need to bring expensive gifts to a woman in order to believe she'll like you or even accept you? Or do you need to offer sex to be liked and pursued by the opposite sex?

What characteristics are important to believe in yourself and are essential to begin your conversion to an authentic person. First, you must begin to overcome hiding who you are. Following your new openness and wish to change, you can start by evaluating whether you are a caring person? Are you fair-minded in dealing with others in personal and business matters? Do people trust you as a responsible person? Are you concerned about your community? Do you care about the wellness of the poor, people in need? Are you willing to teach the young, not only your own children but others too? In other words, do you expend your primary energy in giving to others rather than be self-serving?

All these qualities can be developed through consciousness, and your willingness to change. Character can be built. One of the marks of a great story, a great book is reading of the struggle of a main character as he changes, grows, expands, reaches out to others. We watch leaders who make such changes and also watch leaders who change for the worst, where bad, even evil qualities take over his personality. The acquisition of power can be a major stimulus of change. The direction of change is often determined by what has been hidden and what rises to the surface.

What specific steps can you take to rise to become the person you desire? Hopefully, the direction is one of kindness and giving to others. It is easy to see that scattering clothes over a house and expecting a wife or housekeeper to pick things up is childlike and putting the wife into an inferior position and that the relationship is not equal and not bound by love and a sense of equality. In other words, growing up must be on your agenda.

One important element in change is doing and saying what you mean. Believe in yourself so your actions are real and you believe in them. You must strive to become an honest person to yourself. You are the one determined to become real and authentic. Your challenge is to commit yourself to integrity. These challenges can be met and you can change. Character can be modified as I hope I have indicated. Your sense of self, almost like an awakening into a spiritual life, is in your hands. There is special joy in being authentic.

33

I Don't Remember; Just a Senior Moment?

"I just can't remember your name. Am I embarrassed? Must be one of the old age things. Nothing personal."

"But Johnny, I'm your sister. You must be joking."

"Of course, that's it. I'm just joking. Hi Sis. You're looking great; beautiful as ever."

"Johnny, please get serious. You know I'm not your sister. You do, don't you?"

The above dialogue is written playfully, but unfortunately is a variation of what goes on in the lives and memories of some older people.

We give these lapses, names like **senior moment**, **temporary memory lapse**, or **I wasn't concentrating**, because they are very common and rare is the person who has not scratched his head hoping, even praying, that the name or even the recognition of a person pops back into his head. Many people have developed skills in hiding their temporary lapses by immediately addressing the person through humor. 'Hiya, buddy, good seeing you,' or 'hiya beautiful, you look good enough to hug." Often hidden is an underlying fear, I gotta remember. I can't have Alzheimer's.

Since Dementia in its various forms is generally diagnosable and would be recognizable, I'm assuming that most of us, including me, have these temporary lapses as part of normal memory changes. So, I'm going to address the real issue of this article and that is to offer many ideas that will definitely help many of you to improve your memory and thinking ability.

As a starter I must emphasize that physical exercise, especially aerobic forms, is especially effective in improving and maintaining physical health and the mind's vitality. We all need to get out and walk, swim, dance, ride bikes, play tennis, swing your golf clubs and other activities to keep moving. Definitely good for our mind and bodies.

Energizing the mind occupies a grand arena of ideas, activities, and beliefs. No one article can do justice to the many methods of improving your memory and cultivating a more adventurous mind. But I do have favorites. The simplest and very helpful technique is to REPEAT what you want to remember. Repeating a name or title or a song or quote from a poem, reaps rewards. When you meet someone new and are introduced, REPEAT the person's name. Out loud. "Joan, I love your necklace."

Make a mental picture, that is, VISUALIZE the person's face to fix it in your mind. Some people are able to visualize, scenes, words and pictures. Do it. Try it, especially if this is new for you. Practice visualization. Example, when you take a walk, visualize a scene of flowers, trees. If you do this, please stop walking so you don't stumble when you're practicing.

Some of the other techniques include linking ideas together by association, through words or pictures, making certain that the new ideas connect to something well known or self-evident. Example, linking memory of a newly seen statue with a famous one. Some recall movies or stage plays in detail by keeping previous scenes in mind as the movie plays on.

Another entire area of improving memory and mental alertness is playing games, such as: chess, bridge, crossword puzzles, sudoku, matching words and pictures, finding hidden cues in pictures and putting together difficult picture puzzles.

Many of us create checklists for many purposes, such as: shopping, searching for items online and vacation planning. All to the good. However, to improve your memory you should then try to memorize your lists and follow your memory using the lists only as backup. Today with the use of cell phones and computers there is little reason to memorize anything. Yet memorizing phone numbers is good practice.

Also, it is useful to go over a number of additions and subtractions, as well as multiplication exercises daily. It takes only minutes but does help to keep your mind sharp. What is 18 + 17 or 14 X 7 or 147 – 27. In the past such arithmetic puzzles were simple to do for most of us. Today? Try it and see.

Another way to improve memory, thinking and concentration is writing down summaries of articles and books you have read. You can also answer questions you derive from these readings, which enhances your ability to reflect, think and concentrate. Try doing it out loud.

By doing many of these exercises daily you should improve your memory, as well as your ability to learn, become more creative and of course, become and feel much younger.

I imagine that some readers may prefer to do these exercises with others. Group interaction can help many benefit more quickly. Solo learners may set up a practice schedule, always recognizing that many of the exercises and activities are done spontaneously, such as when you meet someone new. Now is the time to have fun in the process of growing younger.

34

Your Soul Soars With Music

The songs still ring in my mind. A melody of magical power and harmony that stirs my body and envelops my soul. The final notes of Bach's b-minor Mass have never ended. Nor will they or can they. My bliss has reached the state of a spiritual uprising.

Yes, music has that immense power that at times can become overwhelming.

If we need any evidence of the belief in the viability of God it is the ability of humankind to produce music. All kinds, all styles, from hip hop to classical, from Cole Porter to the Beatles to George Gershwin to Bach, Beethoven and Verdi.

Music, especially the music of the great classical composers, has brought a spiritual element to the listening of music. Anyone hearing the great Bach b-minor Mass or St. Matthew Passion or Beethoven's Eroica (3rd symphony) or his Fifth or Ninth symphonies will never be the same. Once you have immersed yourself in Verdi's great operas or in the Wagnerian music dramas and hear the extraordinary singers sing songs of unbelievable beauty, your life has changed.

The great African Jazz tradition that gave us Louis Armstrong and Ella Fitzgerald, the band of Benny Goodman and so many others contribute to music's power. "Sing Sing Sing" will send you to the stars for the trip of a lifetime. Jazz led to country music, folk and rock and roll; Joan Baez and the music of Bob Dylan, Willie Nelson and Paul McCarty. There is an amazing amount of enduring and emotionally powerful music that would take a lifetime to hear.

What is this mysterious force we call music? It appears in ancient historical data that mankind engaged in music making perhaps even before they established a spoken language. Old artifacts buried hundreds and thousands of years and longer appear to be musical instruments. Certain elongated instruments made of bone appear to be primitive flutes found in caves where they had remained for 40,000 to 50,000 years. Some drawings on cave walls suggest dance and music.

Ancient Music as far back as in Ancient Greece, Mesopotamia, China, India included harps, flues, double reed clarinet like instruments and somewhat later percussion instruments and lutes. At some point harmony was established. Dance and singing became commonplace. As the common era unfolded music was incorporated into religious ceremonies and quickly advanced with complexity.

We are very familiar with the astonishingly beautiful music from the eleventh century that is still played today. Medieval music dating from 500 CE to 1400 CE set in motion many of the rules of composition and widespread instrument improvement. During the Renaissance from 1400 to 1600 sacred music, such as motets and masses, was prevalent, leading to the Baroque period dominated by Bach who lived from 1685 to 1750. Secular music followed and the Classical period gave us Haydn and Mozart and led to the Romantic era brought to life by the great Beethoven. The 19th century saw Chopin, Berlioz, Schubert, opening the way to Schuman, Brahms, Wagner. The 20th century led into the Modern and Postmodern period with Mahler, Stravinsky Shostakovitch and Prokofieff.

Thus in a relatively short time we opened our world and minds to the glories of the music that nurtures us today. Millions of people are engaged in music making and creating songs, harmony, and melody. The Internet is filled with sing along, articles on the craft of composing and participating in music making.

Everyone can reach into this musical world and compose. Start by humming or singing a known melody or make one up. Even those who are tone deaf can do it. Now continue the melody with original words added. Any words, be adventurous, within minutes you can be singing a love song, a ballad, a story of grief or loss.

You must accept that this is easy to do. You can become a songwriter. If you persist you might be able to sing original songs for your friends.

Open your hearts and sing out to the world. To a melody of your own or one you know, your words flow easily and absorb your soul. Sing of love and morality and universal truth. Burst out in song; your melody will ring. Your song is upon the earth.

YOUR SONG

I came upon my lover to be,
From yonder mountain peak I did see,
Standing so still but viewing me true,
Before me I now had my cue.

I waved, he smiled; we danced around,
Until in a heap we both went down,
Laughing and gleeful our bodies merged
I knew for certain that we had converged.

Oh what delirium! What joy at last!
I've waited and hoped for many years past,
For love to reach out to claim my soul deep,
For I know this is forever to keep.

35

Conquering Negativism

A cloud overhangs our entire life when negativism remains active in our mind. Negativism destroys peacefulness and the ability to truly love oneself and others. Negativism may appear in various guises. Finding fault in people, being unable to rise to joy with others when your negative feelings come to the surface. Feeling depressed or guilt ridden or self-doubting may be your expression of negativism. These feelings may persist at all times or may only appear during specific or disturbing periods.

Living with an ever-present feeling of criticism about your life and the lives of others is often a clue to the dominance of an inner negative belief system. You need to find ways to lead a positive lifestyle.

Why does negativism persist after the incident or attitude that caused it has passed? To better understand this phenomenon we need to put ourselves in the mind of an infant who is totally dependent on his mother (caretaker) for nourishment and for life. No infant is ever free of the feeling and inner belief that, at times, mother was not there when the pain of hunger has returned. The memory of these early events are theoretically forgotten but remain in an unconscious memory and can become the basis for all future negative experiences.

Depending on intensity and frequency of such experiences a strong feeling of negativism may evolve into a permanent aspect of an individual's personality. Slowly, it colors the lives of people who see life in dark tones with a pessimistic attitude that surrounds their experiences. Many people live and die without making any attempt to cast aside the boundaries that have inhibited their behavior. They have curtailed their activities much of their lives and expect the worst.

They might have been afraid of flying, driving in crowded areas or have lived with a social phobia while functioning behind a façade of reaching out to people. Some believe they can no longer learn anything new and even fear forgetting what they know. They no longer trust their memories or even their judgment. They have begun to withdraw into a cocoon. For them life is narrowing instead of expanding. Such inhibitions and negative behaviors need to be stopped in order to prevent developing a diminishing life instead of an expanding one.

Psychotherapy may be helpful for those seriously impaired by fears, anxiety, social phobias, compulsions and inhibitions. If you need professional help, don't short-change yourself by avoiding therapy. It can be beneficial. However, I don't believe it is necessary for most seniors. Instead, with a little effort and a change in thinking and behavior you can learn ways to improve your life. There's no point in carrying fears any longer.

You're now in the final period of your life and you want it to be as fulfilling as possible. You need to decide that the emotional baggage you have carried is no longer welcome. Here are a few suggestions that anyone can use to become freer and more self-directed. **You have to carefully assess your attitudes, thoughts and behavior.** Unless you are clear about what's bothering you and what you would like to change little can be accomplished.

To overcome a negative mindset that includes low self-esteem you must examine your specific reasons and causes behind your negativism. Here are a few factors that frequently play a part in negativism: guilt, self-doubt, inferiority in one or more areas, such as, intelligence, courage, strength and looks stand out. Try to ferret out the reasons behind your beliefs. By working to overcome your specific causes and determining to use positive thinking to overcome the factors in your negativism you can initiate changing who you are.

Becoming a positive thinker is making a mindset change. Using meditation, mindfulness, mental imagery, affirmations and determination will foster change. Feel you are loved and trusted. You must reach out honestly, openly with friendliness. Share your knowledge. Do whatever it takes to connect with others. Slowly a true belief in your integrity will occur and you will begin to control your life. A positive lifestyle will evolve. You are changing your mindset or belief system.

Belief systems or mindsets involve mental attitudes that determine who we are, how we function as human beings, what we do, how we treat ourselves, how we treat others, and even how we treat the world we live in. Make certain that your belief system is positive and not negative.

Positive beliefs include high self-esteem, loving yourself and others, feeling that you are loved and admired, trusting yourself and enjoying sharing your knowledge. Having the belief in your own integrity and ability to control your life is one that governs most other beliefs. Your positive belief will help you achieve your goals. Remember, you are still learning and growing.

36

The End of All Negatives

Everybody clap your hands, tap your toes, pucker your lips and smile, smile, smile. This is the day you rise above your cares, woes and sorrows, the day that all your pressures have left you for good. Now we fly with the birds and go the way of angels too. We are Rossmoorians to the core and we live that spirit accordingly. Listen, my friends, and go with me on an endless and magical trip. No one here can falter again or bow to the headstrong wind that waits ahead. Reach up and touch the stars as you absorb their celestial light. What do we do in such a moment as we now feel and share? We blow to the wind and hang out with God, together as a single soul. And so, my friends, we live with might in our hearts, pride in our being and love in our soul.

From company to company, from club to club, from handshake to handshake, from friendship to friendship, from family to family, from kiss to kiss and love to love. We launch together in formidable array. We are the Rossmoorians, might I say, once more.

Today, I write our personal preamble to that day in our lives when we have cast aside our negatives, our doubts, any tendency we have to lurk in the past and suffer from memories long gone. Today we search our minds for all the "ifs" and "buts" and "if only." And don't forget the "I'm a failure," and "why did I have poor parents and why did I choose the wrong profession or job or marry the wrong person, live in the wrong neighborhood or, or, or." Today you write FINISH to ALL NEGATIVES.

I hear your words. Sounds like the perfect antidote to my feeling unhappy. I can become a happy bug. Just wait a second, not so fast. How do you expect me to jump on your bandwagon and fly with the butterflies?

OK, Good Question and naturally, you expect a wagonful of ideas to lurch you forward into the world of wonder and glory. Sit tight, I'm starting to dig into my box of mystery tunes to find the one to start me singing. Let's see. No that one belongs to Verdi, that one is Gilbert and Sullivan. Hmm, George Gershman, Rogers and Hammerstein. Finally, the perfect one. It's the Beatles. Do you think they would mind if I used their Yellow Submarine to help me find that elusive song? Don't tell, but I hopped in and I found it, the song we shall all sing and poof, the end of all negatives.

"Negatives, negatives where are you?
Come out and face your due.
I'll fight you and crush you for evermore
All I can say is hee haw, hee haw."

That's it folks, that's it! Sing the song to any melody, loud, proclaiming your new virtue of being negative-free to the world. Feel it, love it, fill yourself with the positive energy you are generating. Kick up your heels, you donkey you.

I'm heading back into the Yellow Submarine for a cup of tea. Guess what! I found another song for you to sing. This is a humdinger. Once you sing this the idea of negativity disappears for good.

"Love, love, love fills the air around,
The sounds spread through the entire town
My mind awakens and screams hello
Love, love, love, that is what I know."

Well, I guess I said it all and time to say goodbye, but just a moment, I do need a refill on the delicious tea so back into the Yellow Submarine. I'll be right out. Don't go away. I've got to say, "I love you all."

Another song, another song. Everybody must climb into that Yellow Submarine for a cup of tulip, rose, dandelion tea and maybe you'll find your own song.

But here's the latest one that clearly nurtures your soul as you sing of returning to the mystical world of the forest and reaching out to the trees that speak wisdom to us and sing of love and closeness and welcoming us into their world.

"Touch me deeply, enter my soul,
Live with me and fill me whole
You are me and I am you
Inseparable lovers we are true."

Folks, you must fall in love with a tree and live in a state of wonder. Your life will bring you joy and you will live in peace. These words will fill your heart and color your world. Imagine for this moment that all worldly negatives have disappeared. Your imagination can lead to new truths. Yes, I am a dreamer and I believe my dreams. My friends, you too have taken that step. Your dreams have become your new reality. We Rossmoorians are on the march. Dream on, my friends, dream on.

37

Shake Those Bones: You Need to Play

Step along and sing and dance, and rattle those bones all day. I wish you all to sing along and spend your time in play.

Grab your **wishbone** and pull it strong and make your wish come true. Bounce it high and swing it round till you reach the clouds. Dream away in every way, your dream will have its say. Do I dream too much, should I bite my tongue or flip upon my head? Does anyone really know what I truly said?

Or prop up my back with sticks and spit, my **backbone** won't ever bend. Nothing I say will be hard again and no mountain will block my way. I'll fight all the demons, and spooks and ghosts and wave them all away. I'll kick and I'll punch and beat them all into a bloody pulp. I'll stand at the top and crush my foes by just moving my little toe.

You think that just can't happen you've got a big guess, as I tell my story too. You have got to laugh and shake your bones at all that I can do. Laugh as I do, hard as you can and shake those bones again. Listen closely and you can hear a tinkle, squeal, or screech. Ha ha, my friends, it's coming at last, the words that make my talk. So pick up your drink and raise it high and read the words ahead. You'll rattle your bones with perceptions anew as you gawk at what I said. Enough, I say, for now we go directly to your head.

After that long and screwball introduction to my words today I'd better find something worthy to say. My editor must still be shaking her bones and wondering if my sanity's at bay. I've got to settle down and write some words that you can take home to bed. This column's about health, I must recall, you heard what I just said.

Laughter is the subject of today's good words. Laugh with all your might. Find any excuse to let out a laugh from a giggle to shaking the earth. Laughter relieves stress, boredom, and all, and tickles your immune system too. You already know that your heart rate goes up when you belly laugh. Your blood pressure too rises a while and then comes crashing down. When you have uttered your last and loudest guffaw, you may even feel spent and relaxed. Your blood pressure now down may even stay down for hours that never end. If you continue to find ways to react to humor it can be a method to facilitate reducing your BP for good. As with the heart many of your body's systems and organs are stimulated by laughter as with any exercise. But laughter adds that moment of pleasure, even joy, and results in good feelings that you carry with you for many minutes of fun. What better medical treatment can you wish for and it's free.

Laughter stimulates your muscles, endocrine system, and increases the production of endorphins. Thus, it also reduces pain, anxiety, depression and general sadness. Does a person readily laugh when depressed? Not usually. However, that person can be stimulated by an empathetic person who finds the right subjects and timing. Laughter can help a person turn a corner, break through a barrier, cope with difficulty. Dance and sing and laugh at will.

Recently laughter has accompanied cancer treatment and rehabilitation programs as a facilitator for healing and as a way to increase oxygen input.

If you are finding it difficult to get into the mood of humor then check out humor online, in book, cartoons, comedy acts and movies. Many old-time movies of *Charlie Chaplin, Groucho Marx, Buster Keaton*, and more recent ones as *Monty Python and the Holy Grail*, or *My Big Fat Greek Wedding* are great mood changers and put a positive charge in your lifestyle. Some TV sitcoms are perpetual humor machines as is the venerable *SNL*.

What better way can we spend our day than conjure up laughter at every turn. Whether the wheel turns forward or backward, up or down, laugh my friends, laugh. If you laugh too hard and your chest begs you stop, slow down awhile, that's all. Start anew with a chuckle or two and you're back in the laughing game. Whether you eat alone or with others galore, laugh at the bean that fell. If the asparagus tries to crawl on your lap swallow it whole with a bite. If the TV is dark and won't light up, make up a tale of woe, and laugh till you cry and run outside, just go. That's it my friends, I wish everyone well and to never stop shaking your bones.

38

Say No to Procrastination

---

*"Our doubts are traitors, and make us lose the good
we oft might win, by fearing to attempt."*

— William Shakespeare 1564-1616. From *Measure for Measure*

Are you one of the otherwise happy people who just can't seem to get rid of all the negative feelings they carry around and never seem to get started on new projects.

Let the above words of William Shakespeare's delightful play *Measure for Measure* inspire you to overcome any tendency toward procrastination, fear of initiating change and hesitancy to move forward.

"What can I do?" you might ask. "There are many ways of changing attitudes and starting on new paths. First is recognizing the importance of becoming an optimist, a person who believes in positive changes as he/she moves into his/her future. A person must overcome any tendency to assume that past behavior and negativity, which are critical components of procrastination will automatically continue in the future. By recognizing your negativity, which is not always so obvious, you will have taken the first step toward change.

Negativism comes out in self-doubt. Not believing in your capacity to initiate change even in limited areas. Recall how Hamlet anguished and fought himself as he felt his reluctance to pursue his revenge against Claudius "O what a rogue and peasant slave am I ..." he said, as he struggled against his procrastination. Later, he believed that the world around him put obstacles in his path. "How all occasions do inform against me..." he cried out. But, as before, his own failure to hold the reins of his life in his own hands resulted in the tragic conclusion leading to his death and that of his mother, as well as the death of Claudius. Finally, he had acted but only after he had lost control of the final events of his life. We have learned that we must gain full control over our actions. Procrastination must end. Judgment alone must determine our actions.

Negativism appears in feeling inadequate or inferior in some area of your life. It often appears in certain actions or lack of actions that limit your life. For example, by saying to yourself that you can never learn to use a computer you have cut off an entirely new approach to advancing your life. Such feelings are equivalent to denying your inner strengths and doubting your ability to compete in the world. This can lead to feelings of inferiority or isolation and relegate you to a lesser role or activity than otherwise might be.

Negativism is often revealed by holding on to the past. By recalling the past or using the past for anecdotes of your life, even if positive, tends to hold people tied to past memories, which often include negative ones, such as being criticized, abused or belittled. Likewise, remembering and dwelling on how you were loved tends to establish a kind of dependence on childhood feelings and may inhibit one from moving forward. Recalling the past is primarily useful to gain insight into current behavior. Repetitive symptoms are almost always tied to past conflicts. Keep your feet solidly planted in the present and future.

Negativism often comes out when believing you have no talent, or physical agility or the mental capacity to be creative. All are inner obstacles to becoming positive and creative or feeling fulfilled. Such obstacles arise when you begin to measure your accomplishments and creativity and feel you are a lesser person than people around you. The rule that will help you overcome such feelings is to NEVER compare yourself to anyone. Believe in your individuality and uniqueness. We all encounter people that can surpass us in anything we can do. So what. We're all unique and need to travel our own path. We can travel in groups or travel alone, but we must believe in our uniqueness.

Many of the most creative and successful people have also felt at times that they were inferior or not talented or creative and lacked the capacity to rise above others. However, they fought their negativity and never believed in their incapacity. In becoming yourself, you do not strive to rise above others. Establish goals that are real for you and strive to attain a goal that is just slightly higher than you believe and go for it. When reached, establish a new goal just slightly out of reach. You will be amazed at how you will change your perspective and attitude strictly by acknowledging your uniqueness and leave negativism out of your life. Don't doubt yourself. Always be willing to attempt reaching forward toward any goal you desire.

Remember Shakespeare's words, "Our doubts are traitors, and make us lose the good we oft might win, by fearing to attempt."

39

Songs of the Soul

Free your soul to wander and ponder the ways of the world. Listen closely as you hear the songs it sings. So much lies hidden away from our searching eyes that revelation will awaken an unknown you. We are like the tiny calf that is born on wobbly feet and lurches around seeking newfound stability and finds his mother standing nearby with love in her heart and milk in her breasts. In moments there is change and the calf is transformed. All creatures who come from darkened recesses suddenly see and we call it birth.

Can birth be a perpetual process of endless growth? Yes. We merely have to revise how we understand growth and replace the concepts with transformation. A flower grows, but a tadpole becomes transformed. A larva grows and changes twice and becomes doubly transformed. Butterflies start out as worms crawling on the limbs of trees and eventually fly into the skies. Babies grow into adults and transform into writers, painters, poets and the maker of songs.

Today, I am reaching for magical words to awaken all of us to stretch our limbs into new and wiggly creatures. When you next seek recognition in the mirror your world will change. You see staring back at you Ariel, the delightful sprite or perhaps Puck, mischievous and unpredictable elf. Or someone unknown and linked to your own spirit. You make a wish with a power to realize change and you march off to a new destination.

We can all do that. What do you want to accomplish that has lain dormant? Today, a new determination has gripped you and grabs you by the hand and pulls you toward discovery. That is you, the new and endlessly seeking you. The couch you once sat on now is filled with prickles and pebbles of discomfort. "No, I no longer want to sit there," you exclaim. The couch reaches out its tenacious arm, flails hopelessly at you, screaming, "You belong to me, sit on me, don't leave me."

But today, you laugh and brush away its efforts, for the songs of your soul have assumed a deep grip on your behavior and have given you a new vitality. When you do look in the mirror you see a person of aliveness and bouncing delight. "My God," you joyously cry out, "Is that really me. Have I truly become renewed?"

What has now happened? As you have listened to the poetic songs of the soul, you have taken charge of your life. You opened the door, peered inside and shook free of the tentacles of the past that have kept you imprisoned. Whether by will or believing in your affirmation of change or undergoing a careful system of inner learning, you heard your songs. The butterfly doesn't ask the crawling worm how it will initiate the transformation, but it trusts that the process will take place. Somehow you also trusted something in yourself. I do not have to spell out what method you used. Does it matter? I wanted to paint pictures. I learned about color. I wanted to compose music I learned the scales. I wanted to sing. I opened my mouth wider and came to understand how my tongue and lips changed the thrust of air and I was singing.

Today when my life is so different, I can still remember looking in the mirror and closing my eyes at the image that stared back. My old self scowled and scolded and accused me of idleness. I screamed back and said it was a coward. "No," it quietly emphasized, "You are the coward and you deserve scorn. If only you would listen to the songs of your soul, you will someday claim the mirror as a loved friend."

My old self now paused and spoke of its sad past when it had looked at the world with tears in its eyes, unhappy, alone, loveless, and friendless. Finally, with great effort it sang a song of such purity and melancholy, that it touched the inner hidden heart of the face it saw and said it is time you ventured out to find yourself by finding friends. Go to places where they wait for you. They want to meet you and welcome you into their midst. The song sang of how sadness became joy, the ways you are drawn to each other. It told of a walk in the forest with others to share, and dancing and whirling about in the hands of another. Your soul sang of the ways you came to love and reaching the ultimate happiness.

One day with happiness in my heart I went to say hello to my mirror and to my utter surprise staring back at me was a face of pure delight singing a song of the soul.

40

The Art of the Bounce

Being able to emotionally bounce back from mishaps, periods of failure, reactions to the loss of loved ones, actually from any negative event in your life is a worthy habit to cultivate. We all admire a person who is resilient and essentially capable of maintaining an optimistic life while going through the ups and downs of existence. No one likes to lose anything at anytime. Maybe it's OK with some games, but not money, love, or possessions. Losers frequently become depressed, excessively angry or withdrawn as they nurse their grievances.

Others, the optimists, quickly assess the meaning of the loss and take whatever measures are needed to correct the situation. They have remained positive and believed in their ability to rectify the situation.

Living in communities with upward mobility, and where opportunities for higher education and social advancement exist establishes a positive attitude in children. When a child grows and sees little opportunity for advancement, a bitterness and resentment may guide his life. Instead of a natural resilience based on optimism, such a child's development may be based on anger and resentment. Arrogance may become his driving force.

How does one become a truly resilient person and positive thinker who is capable of bouncing back from negative situations? For a start we can recognize that those who rarely bend under the weight of traumatic events and seem to have a reserve of energy, become leaders, mentors and the CEOs of organizations. We admire them. Why don't we learn to develop their special abilities that lead to greater resilience? Are these abilities inherited, part of the DNA of certain individuals? In part, our personality is tied to family traits but much of it is cultivated by the social interactions prevalent in these families. Growing up in such families, children incorporate good examples of positive attitudes into their personalities.

For readers seeking to improve their ability to overcome negativism and find a new sense of aliveness and a genuine optimism, there are avenues to take to facilitate such a path. Open your mind as though you were a child absorbing what you judge as positive.

Self-awareness and acceptance of your traits is essential. Consciousness and wish to change are your new weapons. Make them the basis for your new habit patterns. Carefully evaluate your personal traits that lead to pessimism and negativism. Your objective is to overcome these characteristics.

Try to become a member of a circle of positive people. Social interaction where one learns how others remain positive is very rewarding.

Watch and emulate how positive people are both good listeners and good conversationalists. They maintain their presence through alertness, friendliness, warmth, willingness to give and teach and encourage others.

Friendliness is an element of resilience. Cultivate it.

Seek and cultivate new activities where your giving and sharing yourself are welcomed and appreciated. Your self-esteem will increase in conjunction with your expanding positive attitude.

Give freely to charities, help others in need of support, while you spread your assistance to all age groups. Offer to assume greater responsibilities in these activities. By giving to others, you will also be giving to yourself.

Choose certain subjects that interest you and take educational courses to improve your knowledge and potential leadership ability in these activities. Education in general almost always improves a person's self-esteem. Knowledge is power is a familiar and true statement.

Likewise, maintain your physical health through exercise both individually and in selected groups. Selecting a sport such as tennis, pickleball, volley ball, bike riding, ping pong and golf is not only fun but gains new friends, physical skills and health. It can do wonders for your self-esteem.

If certain traumatic or depressing events occur, such as divorce or the death of a loved one, it often helps to seek out support groups. By sharing your reactions and emotions or grief you often gain new insight into your personal conflicts and learn how you can help others by your empathic reactions. A good leader will also help a passive or fearful person speak out and become freer.

Mindfulness, living in the NOW, that is facilitated by meditation, can put a positive spin on a way of life, when you are consciously seeking increased self-esteem and learning to become a more optimistic person. By focusing on your moment to moment attitudes with the specific purpose of overcoming anything negative, you can more rapidly change into a more positive person.

Living in a community of positive, happy, optimistic people who do not follow their calendar age but rather believe and continually try to expand their mental age and social abilities is constructive. It gives you the impetus to change as you identify with your bouncing and resilient neighbors.

41

Conquering Your Worries

Is worry about health and longevity a problem in our wonderful community? Everyone seems to dance and skip along and smile and say hello to the turkeys. Are we all under the control of a special goddess who has cast a spell of prevailing happiness to those who enter our gates? Or is Rossmoor a magical wonderland of cheerfulness and contentment that enters our consciousness once we become part of the community? What is clear is that worries do not belong in our world.

My task today is to make certain that when you finish reading this article all worries about ill health and ending your lifecycle have been left at the entrance gates.

Biggest worries include heart disease, cancer, dementia, maintaining mental and physical health and never losing your enthusiasm for living. Anyone with any fears must focus on overcoming them. Each of us must carefully and honestly, I reiterate honestly, evaluate their level of fear.

Have you accepted that we all live in a lifecycle with a known beginning but initially with no known end time? However, there will come a time when death enters your realistic timeframe. Excluding a sudden accident or an unanticipated fatal heart attack or stroke, you will most likely develop an incurable illness that will bring the end of your life into focus. However, such a situation can be highly variable both in terms of time, pain, required treatment, effect on loved ones and friends and where your final treatment occurs. Having an aggressive cancer that has been adequately treated leaves you with an indefinite future. Have you been cured? Will the cancer reappear? If so, will it again be treatable? This is an area that has created much worry for many people.

Another example is having a heart attack or a stroke and not dying. You are informed about changes in your lifestyle, depending on the severity of your condition and the amount of rehabilitation needed. Much depends on your previous health and lifestyle, your age, the conservatism of your doctor, your level of fear of activity, and your degree of depression.

The symptoms of dementia that appear as you age are highly variable and separating what is real from what is imagined is not an easy task. There is no doubt that the fear of Alzheimer's Disease ranks at or near the top of our worries. As we get older and we begin to have what are considered common memory changes, some weakness and even judgment impairment, it takes little for someone to expand those "symptoms" into impending Alzheimer's. A series of small strokes can appear to be Alzheimer's and brain tumors must be ruled out.

How do we overcome such worries and beliefs that come strictly out of our fears? Always be certain that whatever you fear has been carefully evaluated by a physician and that there is no physical or mental illness actually present. At least you will not be attempting to overcome these worries when you in truth you need medical assistance.

I suggest that you bundle together all your worries; don't hide any of them. They could include any or all the signs of aging. No one escapes getting old and no one escapes dying.

We start by sitting quietly in a chair, eyes closed and taking one or two deep breaths and entering a very relaxed or alpha state. Remain still and slowly think of **every** worry you have. Time is no longer of essence. Make certain you have considered every worry. Now open your eyes and write down all your worries. Go over what you have written down and now consider additional worries, lesser ones or those that had remained elusive and add them to your list. I suggest you do this several or more times. It is always surprising what new worries appear once you fully focus on this state of mind.

Return to the alpha state with full consciousness of ALL the worries you have realized and wrote down and visualize taking those worries and placing them in a strong box, closing and locking the box and carefully storing it in a new corner of your mind. Imagine doing this as fully as possible. The mind's capability to do this comes from childhood defenses of repression and denial. Now put a cloak of invisibility over the box and inwardly rejoice knowing your worries have been removed from your conscious mind. End with an affirmation of total belief that with the power of your mind, you have overcome your worries. Find a sentence or two that reinforces this affirmation.

Repeat this mental imagery and affirmation exercise everyday until you have fully and believably conquered your worries. This works and you will be the recipient of your newfound power and belief.

Now live in peace and contentment.

42

The Bounty of Nature

There are moments when all anxiety and stated toil are becalmed in the infinite leisure and repose of nature.

—Henry_David_Thoreau

Beauty is a harmonious relation between something in our nature and the quality of the object which delights us.

—Blaise Pascal

We live surrounded by the bounty of nature. When we seek beauty or healing or for evidence of God's existence, we unerringly enter nature. No greater healing process exists than being open to the healing properties of trees, flowers and greenery of all kinds. Standing and gazing at the majestic mountains that exist in all parts of the world creates a feeling of inner fulfillment that nurtures us. Waterfalls create awe, butterflies touch the tenderness of our souls. Our spirits soar on the wings of birds and our blood boils with the roar of lions. Elephants and dolphins touch our paternal and maternal instincts. They love their offspring, as we love our children. Nature must never leave us. We must protect it forever. Our lives depend on it.

Today, we go to the many grand national parks in our country and to those in many countries of the world and stand in awe and wonder and try to imagine the forces that created these treasures. Whether you are gazing at the unbelievable vision of the Grand Canyon, or the soaring waterfalls that sparkle in Yosemite, or you are squeezing through the narrow paths of enormous monoliths in Zion or standing under the soaring arches at the Arches National Park you are transported to another world. Have you interacted with those ancient and stately sentinels, the Sequoias and Redwoods, as you reached out and placed your hand upon their bodies and bark? These are the moments of absorbing the timelessness of God's creativity.

I urge you to live for continuous health and increasing longevity. I believe that immersing ourselves in nature is a natural and spiritual way to achieve those goals. Nowhere else can be found the unique moments and everlasting peace and fulfillment that comes from such immersion. Sit against a tree and call it brother and you have changed. Are these words really foreign to anyone? Have you not picked up a rose and gazed into its depths and felt love? A tiny bird flying overhead just out of reach catches your eye and the scurrying lizard darting back into the brush smiled as it rushed away. They have changed us in some indefinable way.

We follow Thoreau's words that *"Nature will bear the closest inspection. She invites us to lay our eye level with her smallest leaf, and take an insect view of its plain."*

Thoreau looked deeply and lovingly at copious morsels of nature that nurtured his soul. He tread lightly upon the soil not disturbing a single insect and brushing off the dust and debris from leaves freeing them to breathe. Thoreau was in love with nature and above all else wanted to share his feelings.

Certainly, your understanding of life takes on a new glow and your connection with nature's wonders is a perpetual high. Hiking along the great trails that take you deeper and deeper into nature you gradually; lose sight and connection with the civilized world and instead enter a dream state. You tune out the footsteps you have taken and walk upon virginal ground. And you are welcomed. No barriers exist. Hands are extended everywhere. They touch you, cling to you, hug you, draw you closer. Nature's love is an ambrosia of feelings.

Walking in nature stirs you to poetry. "O mighty mountain lend me your strength, Bestow upon my mind and body your glorious power. I will live in splendor forever more, A life you give in love's full grace."

Visions arise and glow day and night. Where else will you see stars above the earth and in the sparkle of fireflies and in starfish below the sea. You learn that in nature there is no absurdity, nothing strange or that doesn't belong, nothing that will shatter the hope that there is always more to find. Just as we find more fossils, we find new species. If you need your imagination stirred beyond belief travel over to the Galapagos and speak to a Marine Iguana.

Dear reader, I can go on and on but certainly you need no more encouragement to immerse yourself as much as possible in nature's wonderland. And dream, yes dream, of wonders yet to be. For as your eyes and mind open wider and wider all of nature expands, deepens. The crystal ball sees all. Look and see the celestial vision of the perpetual rose that never changes and yet is always changing. Such is nature's magic. Go out and become the magician.

43

Love to the Rescue

A t 3 AM, low pitched and very soft barks sounded throughout the surrounding condo area. Quietly, singly, dogs of every size and shape emerged from the manors and silently walked toward a small park hidden behind large trees and shrubs and away from main streets. As the dogs congregated noses met, heads shook in welcome and occasional bodies rubbed each other in friendly pleasure.

Without any apparent signal all became quiet, Goldie, a golden-haired retriever, addressed the waiting dogs. To any passerby all that was heard were a few soft barks but to the dogs used to the spoken voices of their owners the words sounded surprisingly human.

"I called this special meeting to evaluate how to help some of our colleagues who are very troubled by the unhappiness of their masters," Goldie said in a low, sad voice. "Chicklet will now report on what's been happening in her home and will include problems from another neighboring condo who also has a dog, who isn't here tonight.

Chicklet, a silky haired Yorkie, looked solemn before speaking. "Mrs. Daniels cries every night since her husband had his heart attack. She is so afraid that he'll die that she never goes out of the house anymore. She hardly ever leaves his side. When he takes a deep breath, she goes to hold his hand or put her hand on his forehead. She looks longingly at the telephone and I know she wants to call the doctor but her husband would be angry. He's so quiet and so nice and doesn't even want to upset the doctor. I try to lick her hand and even jump on the bed and rest my head on my master's chest. I feel so sad."

Chicklet paused then said, "Julie, who isn't here tonight, is almost beside herself, feels terrible watching her mistress, Mrs. Watkins, trying to pretend she's managing by stopping her crying when people come over, but when alone she cries all the time, since her husband died. Julie loves Mrs. Atkins so much. Mrs. Atkins is so upset she hardly eats anymore. Julie is afraid she wants to die and join her husband."

Goldie, obviously upset hearing this terrible news, whined a moment, then addressed the group. "We must have a way to help Chicklet and Julie but first we need to hear from Tibor, who nudged me when he arrived here a little while ago. He was really upset. Tibor, do you feel like talking now?" Goldie asked.

"Yes," Tibor, a large brown Lab, said softly. "My master is so upset she hardly eats or sleeps. As you know I do understand some words and I think she's afraid her granddaughter is going to die. She lies in bed waiting for the telephone to ring with news. She's always afraid when it does and is frantic when it doesn't. Even when I lie in bed next to her it doesn't help much. Although sometimes she turns toward me and hugs me and then she really cries."

"That is terrible. We must find a way to help her. I wonder what her granddaughter is dying of?"

"I hear her mention the word blood all the time, maybe blood disease. I know that word because one day I had been badly cut and they took me to the vet and told them that I had lost a lot of blood. He mentioned the word a number of times and I remembered it."

A deep sadness now prevailed and some of the dogs lay curled up with their head in their paws hiding their eyes.

Goldie finally spoke again. "Let's figure out what can be done to help these unhappy and frightened people."

Buttercup, a little Pekinese, stood and said, "All of these people could benefit by getting out of the house and going for a walk. Let's play our little trick and take our leash to them and then either beg or turn toward the front door or even walk toward the door. They'll think we need to go out and take us. Don't let them put you in the yard instead."

Goldie added. "Mrs. Daniels will then be able to call the doctor outside the house. We have to make certain she takes her cell phone with her. Chicklet, do you think you would be able to make her aware if you see she is not taking her cell phone?"

"I'll try."

"It's hard to imagine how to help Tibor since the little girl in question is very sick. Tibor, your loving nature will no doubt help. I can only say pile it on."

Goldie again went over and touched noses with the dogs in the group as they all left to return to their homes. Chicklet and Tibor couldn't wait to take action.

44

Endless Love

We never truly get over a loss, but we can move forward and evolve from it.

— Elizabeth Berrien

"Those we love don't go away, they walk beside us every day. Unseen, unheard, but always near; still loved, still missed and very dear."

— Anonymous

Many poets have penned lines of love. Some spoke of love that lasted a lifetime. Others of love that came as a flash of light and as quickly burned out. Some ended with love's slow demise and others by abandonment and even death. The loss of love has impelled many of the forsaken to give up seeking love again fearing to repeat the overwhelming emptiness that had made life intolerable.

Love surrounds us and penetrates our souls. Above all, we have learned that love has no bounds, no age, no barriers. Love remains a dominant part of our lives and feelings. Yet so many older people feel alone and that love has disappeared from their lives. Certainly, facing loss of a loved one, realizing a partner has developed an incurable dementia or other illness or increasing anxiety about aging has stirred the fear that love that has nurtured your life will disappear. Your paths in life now appear to open into avenues of darkness. But we are all capable of rising from our most difficult periods. Always consider that the years ahead, often of unknown duration, are years that you deserve to live without gloom or emptiness.

Try to imagine that no matter what situation has given rise to your real or potential loss of love that you can face all such issues internally and know you will have the capacity to overcome them. Don't close your eyes nor your mind to the horrors of an empty life. Face it now. You live in a community where you are surrounded by happy and fulfilled people. No matter your individual status, you will have or can find people to reach out to you when you have opened your mind and the darkness is declining. You will find people with keys ready to open your door. You only need to provide the keyhole.

At times, after loss, your heart remains filled with love. You live in your memories. Frequently, your loss stymies attempts to refill your heart with new memories, new relationships. Sometimes more time is needed to mourn the loss or adapt to living alone. Frequently, many persons now use the new situation to establish a life of solitude and find the courage and direction to rise into a different inner world. This becomes a time of inspiration and, despite one's age, a time of transformation.

Most important is self-scrutiny, evaluating your state of mind, as you attempt to determine if aloneness may be your desired state. Your inner evaluation focuses on all attitudes and feelings, many kept under wraps during the period when your relationship was in focus and viable. Now is the time to rethink your life. Without a conscious attempt to initiate change your life may remain stagnant and your world empty and unfulfilling.

Endless love may lead to greater self-love when aloneness enters the picture. It is time to determine if guilt, fears of disapproval, old conflicts and residual parental attitudes from childhood still impede your personal growth. Understanding the timelessness of inner conflict can open avenues to your repressed conflicts that may still be negatively affecting you.

Can you initiate change when your loved one remains alive though in an altered state as with Alzheimer's Disease or severely incapacitated by extensive cancer or the loss of stamina after a stroke or heart attack? The answer is not clear since it depends on a number of factors that come into focus as the person's situation changes and usually become more difficult to deal with.

By your willingness to allow your mourning or adaptive period to take its course, but with a genuine end point, then change is definitely possible and can lead to major changes in a person's life.

Instead make certain that you are not one of those who live without love. When mental loss or mental withdrawal has commenced and worsened in a loved one, then you need to consciously realize that your love needs replacement. It has become the time to surround yourself with friends, including new ones, and family. In this way you have begun the reaching out process necessary to maintain love. You must overcome any guilt that prevents you from accepting this very realistic attitude. We are nurtured by love. Self-love needs to be maintained. The reality to taking whatever steps necessary to feel loved should never be denied. For some, old relationships provide the love, for others new friends become the essential link and for certain individuals the decision to live a life of solitude satisfies the need of self-love.

45

The Enjoyment of Solitude

Solitude: Time for Reflection, Meditation, Creativity and Peace

---

"What a lovely surprise to finally discover how unlonely being alone can be."

— Ellen Burstyn

"Solitude is the great teacher, and to learn its lessons you must pay attention to it."

— Deepak Chopra

"I love to be alone. I never found the companion that was so companionable as solitude."

— Henry David Thoreau, 'Walden'

"To have passed through life and never experienced solitude is to have never known oneself. To have never known oneself is to have never known anyone."

— Joseph Krutch, 'The Desert Year'

When does solitude enter consciousness and seek expression? Search into yourself and you will know. At any time, in moments of great creativity, when immersed in sadness and loss, when the desire for reflection appears or the wish for utter peacefulness prevails, men and women of all ages may enter the state of solitude.

Solitude beckons some people and threatens others. For many individuals, solitude is likened to being alone and to loneliness. Such perceptions interfere with grasping that solitude can be a constructive interlude in a person's life at any age, especially in the second half of life, when we find that as we age, we are often alone. The need to understand and enjoy your aloneness and solitude is essential to your well-being. Solitude is a state of mind that offers another way of being. It is peaceful and transports you into a different frame of mind and allows you to imagine a new and unique world, a world separate from your usual existence. You can meditate and practice the art of complete mindfulness. You can truly tune into your inner world.

Cultivate your sense of solitude. Learn to meditate. Many people who are single feel that they have reached a point in life that would have been impossible if married or living with someone. They find a special pleasure in solitude and aloneness. Thoughts spring into their minds that are new and awaken ideas and dreams. They become more creative and productive. They have freedom that can only occur when alone.

Others who prefer sharing life with another person don't have to preclude enjoying the benefits of solitude. Being older gives you options to decide on your way of life. There's an art to the practice of being within yourself. Solitude is a special state of mind. Some find periods of solitude rewarding. Through meditation, seeking periods of separateness, even when living with someone, and taking time to be alone can help you discover a new and meaningful part of yourself.

At times solitude is thrust upon us. When a partner in life dies or leaves a relationship, the remaining person is temporarily abandoned. Initially depressed and self-absorbed, the person may gradually adapt to living alone and ultimately may find satisfaction in living alone through the cultivation of solitude. Many times, the adaptation becomes permanent. The person's world has shrunk and once the depression has lifted there is often genuine satisfaction in solitude. Such a state of mind does not primarily mean that a person needs to shun relationships and love.

Some older people choose to be alone and seek solitude. They may decide to not seek new friendships but prefer the connection with nature and animals. Others find that books and art satisfy them and living alone is peaceful and welcoming after a life of conflict and difficulty. Experimentation and a desire to enrich your life is all that's required to determine if periods of time in solitude are for you. Enjoying solitude and intimate relationships do not have to be individually exclusive.

Find time to be alone and learn to enjoy solitude. It will stir your imagination and creativity. It will allow you to find the self that may have been lost as you focused on work, family and friends. It is not meant to steer you into isolation or friendlessness, but to add to your riches as you journey through the years.

At times, sitting quietly, imagine your world surrounded by color, and sounds, sounds that open your mind to a separate world that may be felt as blissful. What are such sounds? Now is when solitude speaks its everlasting song of peace and love. No one needs to be with you or even near you, your imagination in your alone state suffices. Every memory and scene of beauty and wonder can return in such moments and sights never experienced can likewise enter your mind.

You can create dialogues with your inner self or the selves of the great thinkers. You can write a poem and silently sing a song heard for the first time in your world. Solitude is a blessed state of being. Solitude can change your world.

46

Update Your Self-Care

"The greatest weapon against stress is our ability to choose one thought over another."

— William James

"If your compassion does not include yourself, it is incomplete."

— Jack Kornfield

Your health is primarily determined by your steady observation, attentiveness and judgment regarding your level of self-care. There are a number of issues that take precedence in maintaining your health that depend on your unrelenting self- awareness.

Stress is perhaps the most common personal affliction that we face and the causes are almost legion. Almost all activities, illnesses, accidents, social interactions, engaging in sports, creative efforts, especially when the creator faces blocks, doubts and questions about ability produce stress. Family issues, endless conflicts that seem to defy resolution, business struggles, work dissatisfaction and out of control eating compulsions loom large in stress development.

Anything you do to reduce stress is beneficial. Finding ways to improve your family relations and other issues that are major sources of tension in your life are definitely high priority issues. Engaging in pleasant social interactions with family and friends is high on the list to diminish stress.

Exercise burns off tension and should be a routine part of one's daily activities. By reducing negativism regarding ill-conceived politics, or adding your voice to improve personal and local social conditions, such as supporting charities that offer help to the poor, the ill, and the homeless are all stress reducing.

Setting aside alone time for meditation or solitude can lessen stress. Listening to music, reading, watching videos or movies, playing games, walking quietly and being attentive to birds, the passing clouds and trees can help reduce stress.

There are a number of physical problems that can contribute greatly to stress. Allergies have become more intense for longer periods partly due to weather change. Today, in addition to seasonal allergy shots, the use of sublingual tablets or liquid are safe and effective and can be self-administered making your seasonal changes more comfortable.

Orthopedic problems are common sources of discomfort and pain. One of the most prevalent is related to the kneecap and comes from the tendons and ligaments that hold our kneecaps in place or the cartilage under the kneecap that have stretched or torn. Pain around the kneecap can appear for many reasons and sometimes for no discernible reason at all.

Physical therapy and strengthening the muscles that support the knee, such as the thigh muscles, and the core muscles around the hips are generally useful and even necessary. It takes time to heal the knee and to strengthen the various muscles that benefit it. If the problem is a meniscal tear, especially if it is a chronic and degenerative tear, physical therapy may be insufficient and surgery may be needed.

Breast cancer screening has been improved with the introduction of digital breast tomosynthesis and under the advice of your physician you may want to shift to the new screening from digital mammography. The new technique has done a better job of detecting cancer in women of all ages and especially in women with high density breast tissue, which can make cancer more difficult to spot. It works by taking a series of x-ray images which are then composed by a computer into a 3 D image of breast slices.

Recent studies have made clear that missing sleep during the week cannot be made up by longer sleep periods during the weekend. Adults need a minimum of seven to eight hours sleep at night for optimal health. Healing from illness, repair of tissue and organs, rest of all body muscles and reducing mental fatigue require adequate sleep. Don't deprive yourself of sleep. The negative impact is accumulative and the affect increasingly detrimental.

What about the value of naps, meditation, brief rest periods without sleep? Can night sleep be lessened with a daily period of mediation or an afternoon siesta? The answer appears to be "yes." Meditation or a nap for a half hour will supply ½ hour of your daily need of sleep. In addition, daily meditation will also reduce stress.

Do you experience enough beauty in your life? Are you beauty deprived? Is your soul being nourished? Not necessarily the beauty in those you love but rather the beauty that surrounds you. The beauty of nature and of the art and crafts created by your fellow residents. Do you attend botanical gardens and galleries and museums of art? They have been around for hundreds of years but recently you may have possibly neglected them. Your sense of peacefulness and meaningfulness will be enhanced when you seek nature's and art's beauty.

Updating self-care is a testament to self-love and self-growth and is endless in effort and time. You become your own caregiver so raise that glass of wine and celebrate your new sense of youthfulness and agelessness. Listen to your own music as you guide mind, body and soul to peacefulness.

47

Intimate Communication

Intimate communication is a key to a truly loving and meaningful relationship that extends to loving couples, close friends, parents and their children. With perseverance and awareness all couples can improve their understanding of each other and achieve greater closeness.

"Tom, can't you open your ears and listen to me? You seem to drift off or get into your own world, whenever I bring up anything with feelings."

"Honey, what are you talking about? I love to talk intimately where we really get to know each other."

"No, it hasn't happened in years. We talk about politics or the kids, or what our friends are doing or maybe about a movie we saw together. But if I bring up some troubling thought from my past or talk about a painful conversation, I had with my sister you tune out or usually just cut it short."

Roger shook his head wondering what he was missing. Ok, he thought, no point in pretending I get it when most of the time what she says bores me.

"Ok honey, what don't I get? I admit I'm rather a dunce when it comes to understanding you fully. When you talk about those terrible things that happened when you were a child I just tune out. I think, so what. It's yesterday's news and just let it go and live for today."

"I understand that and I'd like to do just that, but for once I'd like to feel you know what I'm talking about."

"Tell me what to do."

"For example. I've mentioned many times how I felt so inferior as a child and how I suffered when people made fun of me. I tried to make people love me but it never seemed to happen until I got into high school and suddenly I was popular and loved it. But I can't really get over all those years when I suffered. Can you understand that?"

Tom realized that he had almost shut her out as she was talking and finally realized how he never understood her. He just never listened and even tried to understand. Why? he wondered. Am I afraid of suffering? As he pondered this new insight, he suddenly realized that he rarely went back into his own childhood.

In an instance, an image appeared in his mind's eye. He saw before him a pretty girl. He remembered her name, Betsy, and heard her words loud and clear. 'Don't come near me. You smell. Don't you ever take a bath? Everyone says you're just a bore and stink.' He cringed as he remembered her words.

And then other words came back. 'Don't fall asleep in my class, young man. And you're too dumb to go with us. Or you're too weak to play on our team.' My god, he thought, I had the same thoughts as Helen. He then realized that by sheer effort he quickly rose to become a partner in his firm as a stockbroker and how convincing he had become to win over clients. I wouldn't let myself fail, I needed to prove I was the best. I needed to believe I wasn't that kid whom no one liked. For a long time, Tom just stood there looking into space but inwardly he knew that something had changed in him.

"Honey, I think I know what you mean," as he proceeded to tell her all that he had just come in his mind. He didn't understand when his wife looked at him strangely and then burst into tears and wrapped her arms around him and just held him.

"That's what I have wanted all these years. To talk together about what we feel."

They cried together knowing that something had changed between them. Like a miracle, but yet so real. When they parted, they knew their world had changed.

How many of us live in a closed world? Many of our foremost thinkers claim that we live isolated lives. No one ever really knows us. Most of us do not even know ourselves. We shy away from self-probing. A small number use mindful meditation to gain insight into their inner world and use their discoveries for personal growth. Some share their insights, others do not. Writers and most artists, who are loners, do probe their conflicts, but primarily to feed their art, not otherwise for sharing.

In a strict sense we are born alone and we die alone. In between we live with love and with pain. How much we share of our deepest feelings determines the degree of intimacy we achieve with others. The integration of self-knowledge and sharing painful and joyful memories of our past with loved ones is often the vehicle that often leads us to our greatest richness in life.

48

Taking Charge of Your Life

On a recent stroll around the wilds of Rossmoor I came upon one of my most intimate friends that I had not seen for some time waiting just ahead of me. As usual with a wary eye, he watched as I approached him. Unlike most crows who would scurry out of your path, Charlie, oh yes, he and I had settled on a name some time ago, stood his ground. As I neared him, he lifted his beak and squeaked out, "Missed you, buddy. Where have you been hiding?"

"Come on Charlie, it's you who has been missing," I laughed. "I needed you for some advice and you never showed up. I was going to write a column about residents who hesitate to leave their condos when alone and go for a walk along the golf course or on one of Rossmoor's streets or trails. To encourage them to become more active I was going to encourage them to use imagery and visualize walking alone while feeling positive and highly spirited. I would emphasize their need to change and transform themselves."

"What a splendid idea," Charlie said. "In other words, you want people to become more courageous."

"That's it, of course. I want people to be fearless."

"That's a great state of mind. Go anywhere. Fly as high as possible."

"Perfect. I want everyone to be a bird."

Charlie squawked. "OK, OK. I get it. Flying without wings. Imagine how people would feel. Marv, you need to emphasize that people can dream and imagine wondrous activities more."

"Yes, dreaming is the key. Everyone must provide their own ideas to find new ways to improve their lives. Instead of fighting conflicts, learn from them. Instead of right and wrong, learn from both points of view? Include personal as well as social and political ideas. At the same time, smile and laugh. Not always easy in a world where so much seems unreal, where personal principles are twisted and distorted. And we're all growing older living in the fleeting moments of our lives. I find that I need to constantly define and redefine health."

"What is 'health?'" Charlie asked.

"Being physically and mentally well. Yes, But that's understood. Just as important, maybe more important, is having love in your life. Yes. But so many people, all lovable, no longer have that love they once had. I am deeply saddened when I imagine people, wonderful people, alone, often without truly close friends to love, but who still desire the intimacy of love. I strive to find ways to encourage lonely people to seek and to find new friends and lovers.

"I am concerned when people depend too much on medications to feel healthy. Yes, many mediations are needed but it is often very difficult for a doctor to separate real need from symptoms related to emotions. Once on a medication, and so many use several and more, it is difficult to end their use, excluding, of course meds that are given for a limited time period, such as antibiotics. For example, many people go on medications to control insulin believing they have incurable diabetes when often a loss of only a few pounds can usually decrease their elevated blood sugar. Doctors and patients need to collaborate to go this route. I search for ways to give patients new paths to improve their health and certainly understanding when their use of medications can be modified.

"I encourage everyone to have a more active role in guiding their own health needs. Primary care doctors should welcome this collaboration and encourage it."

Charlie peered at me and then hopped a few steps closer. "I have a confession."

"What?"

"I always wanted to be as smart as a raven. I'm kind of like a raven, maybe not as big, but you never hear anyone say, 'quoth the crow,' it's always 'quoth the raven.' "

"Oh Charlie, I feel so badly for you. I think you are extremely smart and you should feel proud of yourself. Think of all the wonderful things you can do. You're like a philosopher and teacher and give good advice to other animals.

"And Charlie, I do want to really come down strongly when I tell you to never compare yourself with anyone. Although a raven is in the crow family, he is different. Everyone is unique. Imagine if I compared myself to other writers, I would always find reasons to feel inferior. Instead, I admire and love good writers and learn much from them and have so much pleasure reading their works."

"Ok, buddy, I get it. Got to leave now, but want to mention that I followed your earlier advice and found myself a new friend to glide around with. Now that idea really changed my life."

"So long, Charlie. Maybe someday you'll introduce me to your new friend."

"Someday, my friend, some day."

49

Are You a Warrior?

"Mingle the starlight with your lives and you won't be fretted by trifles."

— Maria Mitchell: America's first professional astronomer

"Reach out, reach out, never falter," rang the piercing voice of Zeus as he raced across the universe in his chariot of golden light.

That is the voice you must hear. For today is your day to reach beyond your dreams and envision a new you and a new world. Not by chance am I calling upon a God to speed you on your way. No longer will I hesitate to urge you to unleash your fullest powers to succeed in your wildest dreams. I want you to succeed and discover that no matter what you have done there is far more waiting, begging for release.

No longer will you hesitate before tackling any task because you believed it was beyond you. No more. Warriors face any and all obstacles and through power of thought and power of will overcome stone walls that crumble on impact. The warrior will look unwaveringly at every task, no matter how monumental as a challenge ripe for defeat. The warrior seizes the moment, no matter what specific task, and marches forward into the fray. You know what they are. Meeting a new friend. And that marathon you were afraid to try. You shake your head hesitantly at trying to paint a picture outdoors, but now the warrior takes control and plants an easel next to a meandering stream. You raise your voice and roar, "I will paint now." And you paint.

Another warrior wanders through the forest and faces a tree of such magnificence that wonder and love strike deeply. Yes, loving a tree feeds the soul of a warrior. The warrior has fallen in love. Admit it and do it.

Love, yes, that's the goal of warriors. Love in its many guises whether a tiny bird, or a butterfly of captivating colors, or the curious fawn who catches your eyes from across the meadow. Did you say hello? Did it smile? Did you want to take it home and make it your friend. No. Why not? What is your imagination for? Tweak it, then tap it then knock it for a loop. See, that fawn is eating a leaf from your hand. Yes, it is smiling.

Love, that is what the warrior seeks so vigilantly and already sees love in its many colors. The vibrancy of the red rose points the way. He looks far and wide to catch the rose in all its scintillating colors and fragrances. For each rose you touch your spirit soars. The warrior's search for the endless rose is boundless for, to his delight, roses change as they age and open their winged petals and finally flutter to earth scattered by the wind to liven the lives of all creatures.

The warrior filled with inspiring hope enters a forest of his imagination and sees the cavorting heron seeking a mate, and the lion fighting to guard his cubs and the rhinoceros though awkward in gait is tender in love. No doubts remain as the warrior widens his gaze and slowly takes in the view of countless shadowy figures of lovers-to-be. The shadows prance away and the warrior presses onward. The shadows just out of reach.

With a booming voice he calls out and the shadows scatter in haste. Undaunted he calls out again and the shadows waver and back away and he rushes forward into the surrounding forest. With renewed hope and yearning eyes, he comes closer to a shadow with a fluttering shape and another like a wisp of smoke and yet another coiled on the ground like a fading snake. But by now our warrior is on the move. With a racing heart he lunges forward and as he is about to touch the very next shadow it disappears, and before him, he sees an angel of exquisite beauty who shyly beckons to him. And he goes closer and they touch. The warrior has met another warrior.

And that is the history of the warrior's quest. Those who venture forth with brightened eyes and hopeful heart and a believer in dreams cast aside every shadow that does not answer the call. How wide the world and far-reaching the captivating song of the clarion trumpet heard from afar that draws the warrior forward into the magical world of love. Therein lies the heaven beyond the imagination, for love creates a nest of such allure that once emmeshed none other can endure.

Warriors, listen and sing your song. Seek out the gods who lead lovers to lovers. Gods know the warrior ventures forward with nary a falter. The warrior's heart is filled with the zeal of the brave and cherish love beyond all else. Yes, it's love, love, love that lights the way.

50

Insomnia

To sleep or not to sleep, that's not the question. It's a mandate. Bounce on the mattress, hug the pillows. Sink yourself into a soft bedspread. Make love. Read a funny book. Read a serious book. Don't read any book. Watch the TV. Turn off the TV. How do you fall asleep? That is the question. You think I have the answer? Well let's try and find out.

Sleep is a time for rest and repair. It is also a time when you create adventures. Dreaming. Yes, in sleep we dream. It allows us to enter new worlds, so different that many people wait until nightfall in order to return to their dreams; thus hope to meet that special man or woman for whom they have searched all of their life. Or becoming David when you meet Goliath or Wonder Woman fighting adversaries. Anything can be true in sleep.

What do people do in order to sleep when sleep eludes them? Many use sleeping pills. If they believe in their efficacy, the pills tend to work for short periods. However, it is well known that long term use tends to lead to addiction to sleeping pills. Some insomniacs can only sleep when they have swallowed their "wonder" pill. A sleeper's belief makes it work. Their pill is like a miracle, but not always. So what is going on?

Sleep is a normal part of our physiology. It is necessary for the repair of neurons used in daily living. Without sleep, fatigue quickly usurps our usual active lifestyle. After a few days of little or no sleep a person may have strange daydreams, develop depression, hallucinations, paranoid reactions and trembling. One's mind wanders and fears enter consciousness.

So how do we overcome insomnia? First, it is important to understand the many causes leading to difficulty in falling asleep. It can be a side effect of medication; illness can result in wakefulness. Other causes that influence many sleepers include: stimulating the mind before bedtime through watching TV, reading, exercising; although for some people having a pattern of participating in one of those activities before bedtime does help induce sleep. The need to use the bathroom at night, sleep apnea, chronic pain, stress, worries of any kind and inconsistency in living style are other factors.

In order to sleep it is important to develop good habits, consistency and reducing factors that interfere with sleep. Included are:

1. Regular eating times with dinner not close to bedtime.

2. Learning to reduce stress, with daily meditation, Non-strenuous exercising, such as walking daily.

3. Finding active interests and new venues for adventure that stimulate and satisfy the mind and reduce feelings of lack of fulfillment or productivity. This helps overcome fear of aging and concern with the passage of time.

4. Determining the right programs and time to watch TV before bedtime.

5. Continuing to explore your causes of insomnia. Remember up to half the adult population has problems with sleep, so you are not alone in seeking ways to induce sleep.

Finally, I want to introduce a technique that I have successfully used with hundreds of people over many years. It comprises two very simple exercises using mental imagery. This technique works by changing memories and brain patterns and is very effective when practiced faithfully. Unless you **fully** believe in its power it is useless to try it. The technique is based on positive thinking and the imagination.

Sit in a comfortable chair, close your eyes, take a deep breath and imagine being fully relaxed.

Exercise One. Do three to five times or more each day but never within two hours of actual bedtime or in a car.

Imagine that you have undressed and are ready for sleep. You see yourself lie down and immediately fall asleep, soundly. Without opening your eyes repeat the exercise three to four times. Then open your eyes and feel very relaxed. The time is about one minute of time. Repeat during day.

Exercise Two: Follow the same directions as above. You can also do in sequence with Exercise One without opening your eyes.

Imagine you have awakened during the night. Get out of bed. Wait a few seconds then immediately return to bed, and lie down and immediately fall asleep.

There is no need to do Exercise Two if you have no trouble falling back asleep once awakened.

You are training your mind to learn to turn off and sleep whenever you lie down in bed. It usually takes a few months to become effective. Under no circumstances, doubt its success. This almost always works. The way you will know it works is that one night you will lie down and within a minute or less you will just fall asleep. Yes, just like that.

Believe in the ability of your mental powers to change your thinking.

51

Finding Inspiration

We love to be inspired. We all admire great athletes who maintain a number one status in their respective sports winning over athletes half their age. And actors still participating in movies in their 80s and 90s are usually very appealing. Michelangelo was carving his last Pieta the day before he died at the age of 89 and that was 500 years ago. Verdi wrote Otello at the age of 74 and Falstaff at the age of 80. He died at the age of 88. Grandma Moses began painting at the age of 72 and painted for 30 years. Beatrice Wood the famous artist and ceramicist worked to the age of 105. Chuck Berry remained singing until he died at the age of 90. Tony Bennett remains singing at the age of 93. Mahathir Mohamad, now 94 assume presidency of Malaysia at age 93, Queen Elizabeth II, the longest governing monarch of Great Britain is now 93. The vitality and continuing creativity at these older ages set in motion our own desire for emulation. Look in the mirror and say, loud and clear, "Go for it."

Is there a secret that accounts for the long ages of such a diverse group of people? I'm still searching for it, but they do have a number of traits in common. They are thinkers and activists. Most strive diligently to become outstanding in their respective fields. They seek methods, learn new skills, desire to improve, generally are willing to share their skills, actively stimulate youngsters to learn and grow.

Not only are we admiring longevity but creativity and enthusiasm. These are people well acquainted with the stars and the songs of birds. Feeling alive and continually fulfilled and never doubting their mental agility are marks of their expansive lives. We strive to enter their world and reach for creative longevity. We must find workable paths to become productive, ways to expand self-direction, enthusiasm for living, belief in the ability to produce meaningful products and develop increasing self-love to want to give rise to our creative products.

Initially you must believe in yourself, develop a clear feeling of self-love, have no doubt that you are capable of producing objects and products of value, if only for yourself. Whatever you do creatively will be fulfilling and there will be no need for the accolades of others. Whether you use mental imagery techniques or just pick up a pencil and write or a paint brush and paint you start the process of creativity. For the sake of simplicity and ease of starting here are a few ideas.

Sit quietly in a chair. Close your eyes. Raise your arm and with your finger as a pencil quickly draw any animal. Don't worry about the details. In your mind's eye you see the complete and realistic animal. In one or two minutes you can draw several to a half dozen animals.

Or how about drawing landscapes. Houses, trees, flowers, children playing, birds flying by.

Want to paint them? Create a palette of several colors and imagine a paint brush that can be automatically cleaned.

Go to the computer in your mind. Log in. Go to Google, find a city, country you want to visit. Walk around. Go window shopping, visit a park, touch the trees and watch the squirrels.

Go skiing. Downhill, fast and furious.

How about paragliding, water skiing, ballroom dancing.

Nothing is impossible. That's the idea. You can **imagine anything** and you can marvel at your skills at taking you into new adventures. Believe in your imagination. It will never lead you astray. It will open up endless new adventures, venues, experiences. You will be overwhelmed by your brilliant mind. And when you finally appear on the stage of the Met and sing Violetta from La Traviata you enjoy the cheers of the audience. Or your painting wins a prize in the local art show, or perhaps, your friends marvel at the beautiful dress you designed and created.

Now it is time to follow your imagination and take a real live step and sing heartily, paint beautifully and design a fascinating dress. From these inspiring thoughts you are now about to convert them into real life experiences, fully involved. Depending on your interests you can study the art and creativity of a highly admired person and strive to emulate that person's style and technique. No different from entering the workshop of a great artist to learn how to paint or sculpt. Initially you work like your mentor than gradually your own individual technique is revealed. From inspiration to emulation and absorbing new techniques to finally entering your own original space. Have fun. Remember you can always stop and play with your imagination.

52

The Joining as I Say Goodbye

The articles that now fill my new book, *Dr. Berenson Pays a Visit* had previously been presented in the Health Column of the *Rossmoor News*. These articles that I so enjoyed writing are now available for readers to review and hopefully to be entertained and informed once again.

In the final article for this book, I am determined as ever to leave you with special ideas to continue to expand your life. I close my eyes (not mandatory), enter my imagination and let my mind wander. I pay deep attention to every thought and feeling, using the power of mindfulness to allow me to float freely through my inner being. That is how I work. That is how I have fun.

Have you ever felt like energy, a form of spirit and know that your body has disappeared, evaporated? How would I know, you could ask? My friend, you must trust and believe your imagination. Anything is possible. From the many ideas that I have thrust in your direction, I have always relied on my imagination and cajoled you, begged you, took you by the hand and together we flew into the sky, beyond the moon and stars. We flew where even the birds have not ventured. This new world gave you a first view of the magic of your imagination.

What a heady world. You became your own director. What power. The nurturance of mysticism. You became an intrepid explorer. No worlds escaped you.

Friends, I want each of you to rise into a new, exciting, even an unbelievable world, merely because you dreamed it. I want to leave you with a unique creation that will stir you forever and make you believe that this book has changed your life. But it is not the book that has changed you. No. It is you, who stirred yourself into the way of the imagination. Once aroused, you can never go back. You are creating your personal magic kingdom. You must promise yourself total freedom and say to yourself that in all the years ahead, "I will be a limitless being."

Your imagination promises this to you.

Merely closing your eyes, the external world can be made to disappear. You can be anywhere, anyone, anything. A lily floating on a pond. A heron gliding under the speckled clouds. An eagle feeding her hungry babies, an astronaut at the helm of a spaceship to the stars or a quiet being sitting in solitude in the shadows of the giant redwoods.

Although I am emphasizing expanding your lives, becoming a limitless person, yet In my final words in this book I finally want to dwell upon our life's end. The ending of our life was a promise made upon our birth. No one at the beginning can surmise the course of his or her life. Do we change the direction of our planet or have we only hitched a ride as an observer? What forces have molded us? Has a teacher guided us or have chance factors planted obstacles in our way that we had to overcome? Had an angel appeared and opened a door for us to enter a never-before seen paradise?

We have had amazing opportunities to learn from the masters, view art from the geniuses of form, read poetry from minds who saw truth often hidden behind the shadows of deception and heard music that linked us to God.

ABOUT THE AUTHOR

I was born in Philadelphia and moved to Los Angeles after graduating from medical school. After a long and productive period as a psychiatrist, psychoanalyst and teacher, spending over fifty years at USC where I also retired as a Clinical Professor Emeritus of Psychiatry at the USC Keck School of Medicine. I was also a Training and Supervising Analyst with the Los Angeles Society and Institute of Psychoanalysis.

I live with my wife, Irene, in Walnut Creek, California. Together we share the love and friendship of six children and eleven grandchildren. Among my many interests are writing, painting, sculpting and composing.

Throughout my life, I have been devoted to all areas of creativity and tasted the intriguing arousal from sculpting, painting, composing music and especially writing. Although I have written during my entire adult life it is only in the past 25 years that I reached that level of creativity and an unrelenting incentive to write that has resulted in my writing almost continuously, producing both fiction and nonfiction books. Words have seduced me and my belief in my imagination has nourished my existence.

I have a deep dedication to creativity, personal freedom and self-direction. My belief in overcoming negativity, finding paths for a positive and fruitful life through the influence of love and the power of the human spirit lie at the heart of my books. I rely fully on my imagination and my belief that my creative muse will always be available to me, an aspect of always having a positive outlook on life.

www.ingramcontent.com/pod-product-compliance
Lightning Source LLC
Chambersburg PA
CBHW061641040426
42446CB00010B/1527